Luminarium
A Grimoire of Cunning Conjuration

Luminarium

A Grimoire of Cunning Conjuration

BJ Swain

Copyright © 2020 Brian Swayne

All rights reserved. This book may not be reproduced, in whole or in part in any form or by any means electronic or mechanical, including photocopying, recording, or by any information storage and retrieval system now known or hereafter invented, without permission of the author, Brian Swayne.

Luminarium
Edited by Suzanne Hill Thackston
Typeset by Brian Swayne

ISBN-13: 9798646317507

Acknowledgements

There are many people who have helped me figure out putting together the pieces that resulted in this ritual system. I couldn't begin to acknowledge all of those individuals, so I express appreciation for those who have helped shape and inspire me as a magician.

Seeing various people put together materials for people to explore during their lockdowns helped inspire me to write this. I appreciate the inspiration that led to writing this text and as well as the warm feeling I gained by seeing people want to make sure that people had things to stay busy and stay connected during their lockdowns. I especially appreciate people who have helped me create multimedia that I've been able to share through YouTube to help contribute to that effort.

Several people have recently spoken with me about this and other writing projects. Their interest and encouragement helped me stay focused while putting this together, and helped me maintain my eagerness to work on other upcoming projects. Joshua Gadbois, Jason Miller, Alison Chicosky, Sarah Clark, Al Cummins, Erzebet Barthold, and many others asked me about this project, asked me about future or other projects, or gave me feedback on Living Spirits. All of them added to the excitement I needed to write this.

I would very much like to thank all the members of my Beta Test Team. They read the draft, they tried the system, they gave me feedback. Most importantly they shared their experiences so that you, the reader, could benefit from them. At the end of the book we present accounts of using the instructions given in this book and what happened when people used them. Alexander, Anneliese, Jonathan, and Aequus in particular gave steady feedback and provided thorough descriptions of their experiences.

I would like to thank my editor, Suz, who I have known forever and who has always been supportive of my development as a magician. Any mistakes which remain, particularly in the materials after the spells chapter, are my own.

Two of my non-magic friends, Aidan and Eric also deserve thanks. Aidan asked me routinely about the progress of the book and encouraged me almost every day to make sure I was writing. He has continued encouraging me in my other projects and has shown consistent concern and support for my ability to be productive. Eric has also asked me about this project and others and went so far as to ask about the impacts and effects of the material presented here. Aidan's support and Eric's interest were both really meaningful to me.

Finally, thanks to Will R. for being excited to join in as the scryer in the original ritual on which this format is based and helping inspire me to plan it. Thanks to Stephanie Olmstead-Dean for stepping in as the scryer when we ended up doing it, and thanks to the participants who petitioned Hoistos and then gave me updates on the results afterwards.

Foreword
By Alexander Deckman

    Most of you picking up this book for the first time will have likely never heard of me, nor should you have. I'm not some famed occult author, or adept magical practitioner. I am just your average reader, to be honest, a night-timing magician at best, who has probably done just as much unsuccessful magic as I have successful magic. Hell, that might even be a generous statement. You may be wondering why I'm even writing this foreword to begin with if I don't even boast a modicum of the usual credentials one finds when reading such a book, and my answer is really quite simple: because, that's exactly the point.

    When BJ Swain, who is every bit of the adept occultist I was referring to up above, asked me if I would beta-test the ritual structure of Luminarium, I was both excited and honoured. I was also nervous, and a bit concerned that I really wasn't experienced enough to be contributing to a professional work such as this. I was fearful that I might entirely fail. To fully address the reason behind me writing this foreword, and not one of the familiar names in the occult community, is that it's quite likely that the reader who needs this book the most, might have similar fears and concerns as I did before testing Luminarium myself. If that should be the case, then all I ask for, is a chance to dispel such fears.

    Without turning this into a Rufus Opus style, "YOU ARE AN AMAZING FUCKING MIRACLE-WORKING BEAUTIFUL REFLECTION OF GOD WHO CAN DO ANYTHING…" pep talk (if that's what you need, then you likely know where to find it by now), I do stand by his sentiment, and you really should too. Doubting your sanctity, and your legitimacy to call upon spirits, Gods, and angels, is just another aspect of the human condition, and it's truly alright to do so, some might even argue that it's sane to do so, until you prove yourself wrong, at least.

So then, what is the purpose of Luminarium? Well, it is to help you, and walk you, step-by-step, toward proving any, and every, doubt of your sanctity, ability, and power to command spirits, commune with angels, and effect miracles – wrong. Luminarium concisely organizes and explains the basic theories behind each essential step of angelic conjuration. It provides spells and applications derived from historical grimoires to further expand upon and develop the format and purpose of the ritual itself. It is not the end-all-be-all of planetary magic, nor is it attempting to be. It is a useful elucidation on millenia-old techniques – written in contemporary language, and in a way that will do more than just help you "get the ball rolling." It can potentially teach you to dial the phone to St. Michael himself.

As I found out for myself, if you dial the phone properly – even if it's ugly, even if you drop the phone, or can't hear them but they can hear you, or your smoke detector goes off while you're trying to talk; if you follow the instructions, Luminarium *will* connect you. Your experience may not be what you expect – in fact most often it probably won't be; but if you've ever doubted that you truly were made in God's image, that you are a spiritual force of nature, capable of miraculous things, and worthy of standing in the presence of the angels themselves, then let Luminarium illuminate your path towards wonder-working. Let it help you prove to yourself, once and for all, that you are every bit of the God on Earth that you were created to be. If I, a Nobody, could do it, then you, certainly can too.

Preface

Luminarium, which means The Lights, or Of the Lights, can be taken as a reference to the planets. As the reader explores deeper, it can also be understood as a reference to the Lamp or Lantern, and the spiritual light that it uses to empower and facilitate your spirit communication.

Empower and facilitate. This book is intended to empower and facilitate you as a magician – as a conjurer of spirits. People believe spirit conjuration is too difficult, too cumbersome, and involves more materials and wading through more literature than they can handle. This will present a way for you to prepare faster and easier. This will present a way for you to conjure with fewer materials. This will present a way for you to set fire to your spiritual vision and ignite the fuse that will lead to an explosion intended to clear away blockades preventing you from being the magician you could be.

The original goal of the text was a short booklet that could be released during the COVID-19 lockdown of 2020. I wrote it fast, but also wrote it bigger than I originally expected. Instead of a long journey with the book, I raced to the finish, writing round the clock. Then for about three weeks a group of magicians read and reviewed it, experimented with it, and helped me edit it. Once I started, I realized I wanted to burn through the process, and get it down on paper, and get it into people's hands as quickly as I could.

Burning through. That's the overall idea.

Luminarium presents a series of magical techniques to empower you as a practitioner. It uses magic to purify you. It uses magic to prepare you. It uses magic to fill you with spiritual fire. Once you begin conjuring it uses magic to give you the clarity of vision to be an effective conjurer.

The book can be read quickly. It's bigger than a booklet but isn't too long, and isn't too heavy on theory and history and the ideas surrounding magic. It's a book of magic, not a book about magic.

The method can be rolled out quickly. The tools are mostly things you'll find at home or can pick up at a grocery store or a Wal-mart. The preparations are easy and effective. The ritual method is simple. It's a 0 to 60mph approach. Even if you don't have a background in magic you could be conjuring spirits in a week to a week and a half.

That's the whole point. So, get reading, get conjuring, get the things you want from magic.

BJ Swain
Catonsville MD
May 2020

Table of Contents

Introduction 15
Preparations 19
Self 21
Meditation 25
Scrying and Occult Senses 29
Spiritual Readiness 33
    Abstinence 33
    Ritual Bathing 33
    Uncrossing 36
    St. Raphael 40
    Mary 42
    Anointing 43
    The Holy Spirit 44
    Hesychasm 45
    Khernips 46
    Recap 48
Tools and Space 51
    Altar (2) 52
    Scrying Bowl 52
    Khernips Bowl (2); Cork or Rope or Bundle of Herbs; Spring Water 53
    Holy Water 53
    Lamp, Seal for the Holy Guardian Angel 56
    Seal for the Spirit 57
    Anointing Oil 57
    Wand 58
    Libations 58

    Red Cloth 58

    Grape Wood/Vine 59

    Magnet 59

    Silver Coin 59

    Pebble 59

    Seal of Solomon 59

    Ring (Optional) 59

    Ritual Attire 60

    Candles 60

    Incense Burner 62

    Incense and Herbs 62

    Stones 64

    Offering Bowl (2) 64

Space 65

Relationships 69

    Hekate 69

    Ancestors 70

    The Elementals 72

        Prayer of the Gnomes 72

        Prayer of the Sylphs 73

        Prayer of the Undines 74

        Prayer of the Salamanders 74

    Daily Prayers 75

        The Headless One 76

        A Prayer From Reginald Scot 80

        Sunday 82

        Monday 84

        Tuesday 85

Wednesday	86
Thursday	87
Friday	88
Saturday	90
Rituals	93
Timing	95
Cosmological Note	97
The Pre-Ritual	98
The Rituals	101
Spirits and Powers of the Sphere of Sol	101
Spirits and Powers of the Sphere of Luna	111
Spirits and Powers of the Sphere of Mars	121
Spirits and Powers of the Sphere of Mercury	130
Spirits and Powers of the Sphere of Jupiter	140
Spirits and Powers of the Sphere of Venus	150
Spirits and Powers of the Sphere of Saturn	160
Pentacles	171
Sol	173
Luna	176
Mars	180
Mercury	183
Jupiter	185
Venus	189
Saturn	193
Spells	201
Sol	202
For Invisibility	202
To Reunite with an Estranged Friend	203

- Luna 205
  - To Appear Beautiful and Enchanting 205
  - To Bring Rain 207
- Mars 208
  - To Separate Two People 208
  - To Heal Someone from Afar 209
- Mercury 210
  - To Open Roads 210
- Jupiter 212
  - House Blessing 212
  - Good Fortune Charm 213
- Venus 215
  - To Obtain Many Friends and Lovers 215
  - To Obtain a Particular Lover 217
- Saturn 218
  - Wash Away Enemy 218
  - To Destroy a Building 220

Recipes and Materials 226

Experiences 230
- Tester One: Aequus 231
- Tester Two: Jonathan 234
- Tester Three: Anneliese 238
- Tester Four: Alexander 242

Introduction

A boom in niche occult publishing, self-publishing, and academic interest in the occult has brought us to a point where we have access to so much more occult knowledge than any generation of magicians in the Anglosphere in centuries. With more communication between practitioners we've also gained more knowledge of living traditions of magic from beyond the Anglosphere.

Since the occult revival we've been told that magic is psychology, authors have told us that conjuring demons conjures portions of our minds. They've told us that when we ask a spirit for money or love we change our outlook and learn to find those things.

Over the last fifteen to twenty years magicians have changed the shape of our understanding of magic, and broken free from the cage of Victorian dramatism. We have more and more magicians understanding magic and the world itself as a living organism. We are encountering a world of vibrant spirits both those recorded in books of conjuration and those living in the streams and trees around our homes, those passed along in traditions of sorcery and those hidden in the nooks of the concrete jungles where we adventure day to day.

Breaking free from the psychological paradigm coincided with the expansion of access to occult knowledge. The return of animism coincides with an increase in numbers of magical practitioners. We now have instant means of global communication which allow people to access the spirit traditions which call to them, rather than simply joining up with whatever flavor group happens to be in their area.

We have freedom, we have information, and we have community, and in having these things we have so much opportunity for learning, growth, and innovation.

Despite this freedom and the gifts it brings us, sometimes it seems convenient to create new cages – to convince people they can't do magic or work with spirits unless they have everything perfectly aligned. Each tool exactly to spec, each word in the correct pronunciation of a dead language, meticulously pulled apart explorations of a singular manuscript until each twitching finger it describes is executed in exactly the right moment in exactly the right fashion. We're told that if we don't reach that level of perfection that whatever spirits we encounter are fantasy, there is no proof that our experiences aren't in our heads. We're told to ignore that the test of magic is its ability to accomplish things with it rather than proving ourselves by our ability to anachronistically copy by rote.

 There is power in repeating things which have been done before. There is a necessity in learning systems as they are before we pull them apart. But there is also magic and a living world of spirits all around us. There is benefit in exploring how various means of engaging that world can work together to give us simpler and more powerful spirit interaction and therefore greater ability to change things in our lives and those of the people we care about.

 With that in mind, this short text will take an approach similar to that of the cunning folk, which is in fact also the approach of most historical practitioners whose records survive in working manuals. We'll take elements of traditions of spirit conjuration and elements of folk magic. We will build and leverage spirit relationships. We'll use magic to facilitate magic. With all of this we will make a simple means of spirit access. We'll present a system through a series of rituals. It will be a system which you can augment and adjust as per your needs and the instructions you receive from your spirits.

 We will work with ancestors as a source of leverage and power. We will work with Night as the source of creation, Eros as the love that binds forces and materials together in order to make magic occur, and Hekate as the intermediary between this world and the spirit world and as the key holder who makes the way for things to come into being. We will work with our own individual guardian angel to illuminate our spirit interactions. We will work with the angels of the planets and the zodiac to make magic for us and with the elementals to shape that magic into being. We will call upon the spirits of time and place to empower and admit the work we are doing.

  That's pretty much it for a cosmology. We don't need a lot more description than that. What we need is to hit the ground running. We need to pick up a handful of simple items, and we need to talk to the spirits to whom we have access. We need to make magic happen. We need to open the door to what we can do, rather than close the door by building hurdles. Once we're jacked in and up and running, we can dig deeper, dive into more systems, and expand what we're doing. This is our simple ideological structure, and now we'll give simple tools, so you can be conjuring within days.

Luminarium

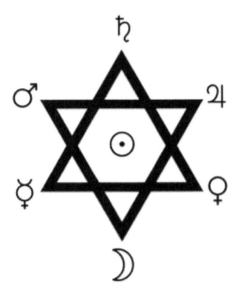

Preparations

Many traditional systems of magic involve a lot of preparations. If we're talking the grimoires we need to build and consecrate tools, we need to purify ourselves, maybe go to Mass if it's an older grimoire, maybe go to Mass, maybe even multiple times. We might need to make tools in order to purify ourselves. We might need to purify ourselves to make tools. We might need to make tools in order to make other tools and so on until we come to chicken-and-egg what-to-do-first scenarios. Once we step back and explore them calmly, they become more apparently doable. They take a lot of investment, a lot of time, and a lot of effort. Sometimes we want to experience something before we do all that. Sometimes we need a solution before we can arrange all that. There is value in those preparations, but they aren't the only way to go.

Still, magic can be helped by preparing for it. We're going to give some options for ways to prepare based on the grimoires and other spiritual work. The more preparation you do, the more benefit you'll have, and the easier magic will be. You can begin with the options we give here. We'll give advice on what's needed versus what's nice. You can expand with preparations from other spiritual systems as you learn more.

We will break down our look at preparations into three groups. The first set of preparations will be preparations of yourself. Some of these will deal with spiritual cleanliness, some with preparing you mentally to do the work. The second set will be preparations of tools and space. There will be things you'll need when doing your work and you'll need a space to do it in. We'll keep those elements simple and we'll use a setup that works for people with limited space. The final set of preparations will deal with spirit relationships and exercises. Sometimes magic is a spell kit we purchase with some pre-prepared tools and words for a simple need and that's all there is too it. Sometimes magic is something done by a magician. These instructions will let you work in that latter context, which means you'll need relationships with the spirit world, not just some tools and words.

Self

When we consider preparing the self for magic there are four elements to consider. First, are we in the right mental state for what we're about to do? Second, do we have the skills we need to engage the experience? Third, are we mentally ready for this kind of experience? Fourth, are we spiritually well-adjusted and in a position of authority to make this work?

For the mental state element, you need a certain level of centeredness. You can't be distracted. You need level of focus. It's also helpful to be relaxed. This might not seem obvious, but engaging the experience works better if you're relaxed and open. You don't want to be in a sleepy dream-state; you need to be alert and aware. You're dealing with things that are real. You need a state of desire. But you can't be keyed up, or chasing after the vision. You can't be overly anxious or attempting to force yourself to experience something. Sometimes you won't see something. Sometimes spirits may not come. That's part of dealing with something real and objective. It isn't always 100 percent successful, because not everything is about you.

Being fixated, or obsessively looking for a result, might just lead you to imagining one. If you're too busy imagining what you want to happen you might miss what is really happening. So, you need to be relaxed enough to allow communication to happen. You need to be secure and honest with yourself enough to realize when it isn't happening. Be relaxed and open, but also be aware and alert enough to perform your actions and perceive the results.

This describes the mental state we want for this particular work. In some approaches to magic and conjuration this may vary. Dream states and the border between wake and sleep can be useful. Agitation and turbulence can be useful. These just aren't what we need for what we're doing here.

To work on our mental state, we'll present a few forms of meditation. These are recommendations rather than things which are absolutely necessary. Experiment with them, see what works for you. If you have other ways of achieving the necessary mental space you can use those.

It's been major work adjusting that view to one in which engaging spirits is the key to learning spirit magic. I came up under the idea that you had to go through all sorts of intense training to be a magician before spirit magic would be viable. Still, having some basic skills can help. The meditations we're suggesting come out of that pre-magical training idea. Put simply, the most basic skill is patient listening. Learn to be aware of your surroundings and be able to feel what's happening. To take it further, scrying and occult sensation are helpful. Spirits do not have physical bodies. They have being and essence but the extent of their substantial nature is not the same as that which occurs on the physical level. When we encounter spirits, they impact our spiritual awareness, which stimulate our minds and creates perceptions. For some people, those perceptions will be very natural and physical; for some they will be visionary. Learning to be open to and engaged with those visionary experiences or spiritual sensations is necessary to this work.

Mental readiness is different from having the right mental state. There is a famous recounting of a man curious to see an experiment of magic, who paid a magician to take him to a stadium and conjure spirits. They brought a horde of magic books, a great deal of incense, tools and a boy. They began their conjurations and the boy described what happened. As legions of spirits loomed around them, they fell into a state of terror and had to expel them. They weren't ready for the experience. Magic causes you to encounter things and have experiences beyond what are part of every-day life. You will talk to spirits, you will gain hidden knowledge, you will change things in your life. You will meet the dead. You will invite forces into your life that will impact you and which may try to encounter you even when you're not the one initiating contact. Consider what you'll be experiencing, consider what you're trying to cause to happen, consider the work, the risks, and the benefits involved and make yourself ready for that.

Finally, spiritual status and authority. This is the big kicker for modern magic practitioners. This is the justification given by many grimoire purists for why we have to engage in various preparations before working magic. If we're not spiritually pure this presents a host of imagined pitfalls with varying degrees of veracity. They say spirits will avoid us, or spirits will not respond to us, or they will take advantage of us, or we won't be able to control them. People have different explanations of what it is to be spiritually pure and what the impacts are. This comes down to our beliefs and our interpretations of spirits and the bases for our interactions therewith. Our modern culture lacks a strong model for spiritual cleanliness, leaving us grasping for our place within a world of spirits. As a result, we grasp at ways to explain this and retrofit our world views to these instructions.

Because of this retrofitting, there is a tendency to demand that an intense level of engagement be enacted from the beginning, then we find excuses for doing less once we become experienced. This could be reasonable, or it could be a way of creating a barrier. Around the world, there are spiritual preparations people undergo for spirit work, so we know it has actual material impact and benefits. Yet there are spirit encounters, both occurring naturally and magically initiated, which occur without all that preparation. So, magic can be done and spirits can be encountered without all those steps.

In my experience, more preparation can create a more powerful and an easier experience. One's own status or condition can also provide elements which create more powerful experiences or facilitate experiences. Effective work can be done with minimal preparation. You'll need to judge how much you need or want. Experiment with it. Find what works. The instructions we give will provide some short cuts, and we'll discuss some of the traditional methods as well. Some things we'll consider a necessary minimum some will be optional recommendations.

My interpretation of spiritual cleanliness and authority is about charism or friction. That charism is a sort of power or force. That friction creates capacitance which provides authority and power. Spiritual cleanliness also deals with the removal of miasma or the impurities which cause distraction and inability.

Preparedness is about capability. When we do things to enter into a spiritual state – ritual bathing, intense prayer, daily rituals, abstaining from foods or pleasure etc. – we create stress and tension in our beings. We shift our focus outside of where it is drawn by the material, and we create a scratching and gnawing of desire in ourselves for both that which we're seeking and that which we're avoiding. We create opposition and motion in our beings. This creates a friction or capacitance which simulates spiritual charism, or the power or grace of spirit, that gives us the power to command occult forces and spirits – as well as the power to perceive them. We create an altered state of consciousness and awareness while shifting our eyes to the direction of the spiritual. Between these two, things the ability to call and perceive is increased. Further, we may have faults, actions, guilt, or spiritual encumberments which draw away our attention or nullify our ability. Spiritual cleansing helps remove these things, both in a real fashion and from our psyche. The psychic or mental impact of our condition and its ability to distract or hamper us is a real consideration. So, we need tools to deal with it.

The elements of spiritual preparation we will provide will deal with these factors, creating opportunities for that friction and charisma and removing the effects, both spiritual and mental, of those things which impact us.

Meditation

We will present three forms of traditional meditation in very simplified forms. If you find them useful, pursue deeper explorations of these from traditional sources or those trained in traditional sources. The descriptions we will give will be enough to get you started, and that is all that is needed for our purposes. The first technique is to help calm the mind and hone the ability to focus and exclude distraction. The second will help you explore your mind, your thoughts, your motivations. The third will help you be present in your space and aware of influences and presences in your space. Each of these elements is necessary to the work we will be doing. You must either spend time engaging these meditations or some alternate practice that achieves these same ends.

Pranayama

The simple form of Pranayama, or breath control, generally taught in magic is to sit comfortably and pay attention to one's pattern of breathing and then assert a pattern of control.

Breathe in for a count of 4, hold the breath in for a count of 4, breathe out for a count of 4, hold breath out for a count of 4.

This can then be adjusted as it goes retaining the hold of four and making the breathing a count of two.

Start with a short period of time, roughly five minutes. Work to about fifteen minutes as a standard. Longer times can have additional benefit.

Breathing

This is the opposite of the breath control. Where that is a meditation of concentration this is one of insight.

Sit upright in a relaxed comfortable position but one which retains uprightness.

Breathe naturally. Observe but do not control your breathing. Observe the body as you breathe. Note the feeling of the abdomen rising and falling with breath; note the speed and depth of your breathing.

While observing your breathing observe when distraction occurs. If you feel a sensation, hear a sound, taste a taste mentally note "I feel warmth" "I hear noise." Do not fixate on the details, just passively observe the distraction and when it fades return to your breathing.

When your mind presents a distraction, do not attempt to concentrate or focus away from it. Passively watch the distraction. Note that it is a thought, but allow that thought to develop its natural process. Do not guide the thinking, simply observe.

When the thought reaches its culmination return to your breathing. Observe your breath and the body breathing.

Thoughts should rise and fall routinely from this. When you are done reflect on the trends in the thoughts which rise. Was there focus? Was there a pattern? Did something cause them? Where did they go?

This reflection can help with our mental readiness in addition to the mental state. We learn to observe what our thoughts sound and feel like versus what other stimuli feel like. We also learn how we perceive. We learn if we have a particular focus or desire, or perhaps gain insight into that or into our prejudices or fixations. These may be things we need to deal with before certain spirit work. Our analysis may allow us to identify why we want to do certain spirit work. It will also help us in understanding what is our own mind versus what is an external spirit stimulus.

Walking Meditation

The description for this meditation is simple but the execution less so.

Go to a place outside and take a walk. Do not walk purposefully or to a particular destination. Fix your thoughts simply on the fact that you are walking. Observe the sensation of your foot falls, observe the movement of your muscles, observe your breathing. Observe all things you encounter, feel, and experience. Continue the thought and awareness that you are walking; bring these observations into the space of the thought that you are walking. Comprehend all elements of the experience, no matter how minute, until you intimately understand that the act of walking is indiscernible from the phenomena you observe.

Luminarium

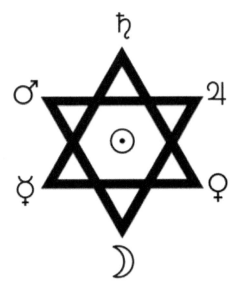

Scrying and Occult Senses

Many have asserted that spirits must appear visibly for a conjuration to be a success, however there are historical magic texts that note that certain types of spirits will not appear visibly, or that a spirit may be present without appearing. Many successful practitioners note as well that the presence and the effectiveness of the spirit are more important than the visibility. There are benefits to visibility and contexts in which it may be necessary or useful. The work we will be doing is with angels, and they generally are not bound to produce physical manifestation or commanded to visible appearance. They may appear visibly, or create some physical vision, or they may engage one's spiritual vision, or simply speak to you.

With any spirit work, whether the spirit is visible or not, the spirit should be perceptible. There should be a noticeable change in the magician's experience of the environment, or within the crystal, or the awareness of a presence, or an interacting force. Beyond that, visibility and mode of communication will vary based on the method, the magician, and the spirit.

There are many resources available which will provide numerous techniques and exercises to develop the magician's ability to scry and to use their occult senses. For our purposes we will introduce the concept and provide a few small recommendations.

Imaginal senses or occult senses are the ability to perceive without physical stimulus. This can be accomplished through training the mind and stimulating perceptions through thought. This can also be experienced by non-physical stimuli such as that of interaction with a spirit or an occult force. To train the capacity of one's perceptions to vividly respond to non-physical stimuli one must work initially through the imagination as invoking unseen forces without the ability to perceive them is less advisable.

To train visionary capacity, build objects in the mind's eye. Once you can hold an object of increasing detail, move on to small scenes of multiple objects. Then move on to creating and furnishing entire rooms. Move through the mindscape and explore increasing detail. It is difficult, but it is also possible to train the eyes to respond to mental stimulus. Typically, this is easiest to begin in the periphery by building detail upon something without detail. Then more frontal vision by changing the perception of smaller details and then working to enlarge them. Sounds and scents are somewhat easier to simulate mentally through recollection. Practice remembering a song, focus on the memory until the ears begin to actually perceive the song. Remember the scent of a food, or of a loved one, or a favorite place. Immerse your mind in that memory until you perceive the scent.

These imaginal exercises will not create magical experiences and are not equated to them. They begin to build the capacity of the senses to be triggered by stimuli acting upon your psyche. While spirit work is not psychological in the sense that spirits are, as magicians once taught, parts of your mind, it is psychological in the sense that – like all experiences; we perceive spirits through the way in which our psyches interpret stimuli.

Scrying will be assisted by these imaginal sensory muscles. Scrying is the art of gazing. It is a form of passive looking that allows us to see beyond the physical nature of the thing being gazed into. Crystals, mirrors, water, incense, flames are all common things to scry. The scryer physically relaxes the eyes and looks passively as if looking through the object of the scrying. Spiritually speaking, they extend the locus of their spiritual awareness to connect with the scrying device. This can be assisted by imagining a beam from the mind to the device and then moving the focus of your awareness from the seat of the head along that beam to the device. Allow a sense of your presence and attention to fall into the device. Don't search after the appearance of the spirit or vision – allow it to appear.

While you are beginning, it may be difficult to develop this capability. Our conjuration method will have elements intended to aid in this. Seeing the spirit is not necessary for working with it. If you experience the spirit's presence and are able to communicate with it that is sufficient. If you can-not hear the spirit, some divination device can be used as a means of communicating.

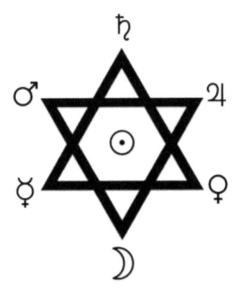

Spiritual Readiness

Abstinence

　　Abstinence, prayer, lifestyle changes, meditation and reflection, these are very powerful methods for obtaining spiritual capacitance, or the friction which aids in spirit work. The body is put into a state of desire, while the mind is fixed upon the spiritual. This creates a certain internal dynamism. We can abstain from any number of things: certain foods, alcohol, sex, swearing, speaking. We can add behaviors such as charity or service work. We can pray multiple times a day, or take on inner mantra work. We can sit in meditation. We both agitate the fixation we have within our normal routine and calm ourselves into a spiritual focus. This is the method the grimoires use to create an influx of spiritual power, the needed state of mental awareness, and the singular focus on the spiritual matter at hand. Three days, seven days, or nine days are common durations for such action; however the time can be longer in some contexts.

　　In all cases, this period of abstinence and preparation is a shortcut used in lieu of a lifetime discipline of spiritual training. In this approach there is definite benefit in adding these times of abstinence and preparation, but they are not required. We are providing methods to stimulate other elements to help in achieving spirit contact. If the magician has the time to engage in these periods, do so, or experiment with doing so. If the magician needs to hit the ground running without weeks of abstinence the methods provided in this text are designed for that purpose.

Ritual Bathing

　　Ritual bathing is a traditional means of purification. It can also be a means of empowerment. Both baths we present will involve cleaning yourself, then soaking in the bath, then washing again at the end of the bath. Begin and end the bath with the prayers given. Continuous internal prayer or contemplation should be attempted during the bath. Either or both baths may be used in preparation, depending upon the particular need.

For Purification

Place in the bath Hyssop Oil. Rose Oil may be added as well. Pray the psalm followed by the verse. The verse should also be prayed when washing before and after the bath.

Psalm 51
(1) Have mercy upon me, O God, according to thy lovingkindness: according unto the multitude of thy tender mercies blot out my transgressions. (2) Wash me throughly from mine iniquity, and cleanse me from my sin. (3) For I acknowledge my transgressions: and my sin is ever before me. (4) Against thee, thee only, have I sinned, and done this evil in thy sight: that thou mightest be justified when thou speakest, and be clear when thou judgest. (5) Behold, I was shapen in iniquity; and in sin did my mother conceive me. (6) Behold, thou desirest truth in the inward parts: and in the hidden part thou shalt make me to know wisdom. (7) Purge me with hyssop, and I shall be clean: wash me, and I shall be whiter than snow. (8) Make me to hear joy and gladness; that the bones which thou hast broken may rejoice. (9) Hide thy face from my sins, and blot out all mine iniquities. (10) Create in me a clean heart, O God; and renew a right spirit within me. (11) Cast me not away from thy presence; and take not thy holy spirit from me. (12) Restore unto me the joy of thy salvation; and uphold me with thy free spirit. (13) Then will I teach transgressors thy ways; and sinners shall be converted unto thee. (14) Deliver me from bloodguiltiness, O God, thou God of my salvation: and my tongue shall sing aloud of thy righteousness. (15) O Lord, open thou my lips; and my mouth shall shew forth thy praise. (16) For thou desirest not sacrifice; else would I give it: thou delightest not

in burnt offering. (17) The sacrifices of God are a broken spirit: a broken and a contrite heart, O God, thou wilt not despise. (18) Do good in thy good pleasure unto Zion: build thou the walls of Jerusalem. (19) Then shalt thou be pleased with the sacrifices of righteousness, with burnt offering and whole burnt offering: then shall they offer bullocks upon thine altar.

Verse: ***Purge me with hyssop, and I shall be clean: wash me, and I shall be whiter than snow.***

For Empowerment

Place in the bath either Oil of Abramelin or a combination of Frankincense and Dragons Blood Oils in equal parts. Pray the following Psalm and prayer to your Guardian Angel.

Psalm 27
(1) The Lord is my light and my salvation; whom shall I fear? the Lord is the strength of my life; of whom shall I be afraid? (2) When the wicked, even mine enemies and my foes, came upon me to eat up my flesh, they stumbled and fell. (3) Though an host should encamp against me, my heart shall not fear: though war should rise against me, in this will I be confident. (4) One thing have I desired of the Lord, that will I seek after; that I may dwell in the house of the Lord all the days of my life, to behold the beauty of the Lord, and to inquire in his temple. (5) For in the time of trouble he shall hide me in his pavilion: in the secret of his tabernacle shall he hide me; he shall set me up upon a rock. (6) And now shall mine head be lifted up above mine enemies round about me: therefore will I offer in his tabernacle sacrifices of joy; I will sing, yea, I will sing praises unto the Lord. (7) Hear, O Lord, when I cry with my voice: have mercy also upon me, and answer me. (8) When thou saidst, Seek ye my face; my heart said unto thee, Thy face, Lord, will I seek. (9) Hide not thy face far from me; put not thy servant away in anger: thou

hast been my help; leave me not, neither forsake me, O God of my salvation. (10) When my father and my mother forsake me, then the Lord will take me up. (11) Teach me thy way, O Lord, and lead me in a plain path, because of mine enemies. (12) Deliver me not over unto the will of mine enemies: for false witnesses are risen up against me, and such as breathe out cruelty. (13) I had fainted, unless I had believed to see the goodness of the Lord in the land of the living. (14) Wait on the Lord: be of good courage, and he shall strengthen thine heart: wait, I say, on the Lord.

Prayer to the Guardian Angel

Angel appointed over me at my birth, come unto me like a heavenly fire. Shine brilliantly and guide me, teach me, and give me the strength to triumph in all things.

Uncrossing

Uncrossing is often thought of as a means of removing curses. More accurately, it removes a crossed condition. Crossed conditions can be caused by someone cursing you in a traditional sense of placing a jinx or hex. We have to remember, though, that in traditional cultures there is an awareness that curses can be unintentional and caused by careless words thoughts and jealous eyes. We can acquire states that affect us like curses through our own misdeeds and through our active work against ourselves. Uncrossing helps untie the knots, or open up the ways that have been closed off by these effects. It can be highly effective in improving our lives. If you are in a state of being crossed, it can make magic and spirit work more difficult or ineffective. With these things in mind, uncrossing can be a useful technique in purification and preparation. If we're engaging in short quick preparations because we don't have weeks to prepare ourselves, this can also be a magical shortcut.

Simple Uncrossing with a Candle and Oil

Strip down. Take a votive candle and "scrub" yourself by rubbing the candle over your body in counter clockwise motions. This can be a combination of circling around the body and circles upon the body. Get your whole body. While doing this, pray that your crossed conditions, negativity, curses, or impediments be removed. If you believe people are actively working to harm you, pray that their efforts turn back upon them.

When you are done, dress the candle with Uncrossing Oil. If you believe people are working strongly against, you dress the candle instead with Send Back Evil Oil.

Place the candle in the western part of the room and burn it. Let it burn down completely, do not put it out.

Pray the Psalm.

Psalm 91 *(1) He that dwelleth in the secret place of the most High shall abide under the shadow of the Almighty. (2) I will say of the LORD, He is my refuge and my fortress: my God; in him will I trust. (3) Surely he shall deliver thee from the snare of the fowler, and from the noisome pestilence. (4) He shall cover thee with his feathers, and under his wings shalt thou trust: his truth shall be thy shield and buckler. (5) Thou shalt not be afraid for the terror by night; nor for the arrow that flieth by day; (6) Nor for the pestilence that walketh in darkness; nor for the destruction that wasteth at noonday. (7) A thousand shall fall at thy side, and ten thousand at thy right hand; but it shall not come nigh thee. (8) Only with thine eyes shalt thou behold and see the reward of the wicked. (9) Because thou hast made the LORD, which is my refuge, even the most High, thy habitation; (10) There shall no evil befall thee, neither shall any plague come nigh thy dwelling. (11) For he shall give his angels charge over thee, to keep thee in all thy ways. (12) They shall bear thee up in their hands, lest thou dash thy foot against a stone. (13) Thou shalt tread upon the lion and adder: the young lion and the dragon shalt thou trample under feet. (14) Because he hath set his love upon me, therefore will I deliver him: I will set him on high, because he hath known my name. (15) He shall call upon me, and I will answer him: I will be with him in trouble; I will deliver him, and honour him. (16) With long life will I satisfy him, and shew him my salvation.*

Alternatively if you believe someone is working against you use this Psalm instead of, or along with the Psalm 91.

Psalm 37 *(1) Fret not thyself because of evildoers, neither be thou envious against the workers of iniquity. (2) For they shall soon be cut down like the grass, and wither as the green herb. (3) Trust in the Lord, and do good; so shalt thou dwell in the land, and verily thou shalt be fed. (4) Delight thyself also in the Lord: and he shall give thee the desires of thine heart. (5) Commit thy way unto the Lord; trust also in him; and he shall bring it to pass. (6) And he shall bring forth thy righteousness as the light, and thy judgment as the noonday. (7) Rest in the Lord, and wait patiently for him: fret not thyself because of him who prospereth in his way, because of the man who bringeth wicked devices to pass. (8) Cease from anger, and forsake wrath: fret not thyself in any wise to do evil. (9) For evildoers shall be cut off: but those that wait upon the Lord, they shall inherit the earth. (10) For yet a little while, and the wicked shall not be: yea, thou shalt diligently consider his place, and it shall not be. (11) But the meek shall inherit the earth; and shall delight themselves in the abundance of peace. (12) The wicked plotteth against the just, and gnasheth upon him with his teeth. (13) The Lord shall laugh at him: for he seeth that his day is coming. (14) The wicked have drawn out the sword, and have bent their bow, to cast down the poor and needy, and to slay such as be of upright conversation. (15) Their sword shall enter into their own heart, and their bows shall be broken. (16) A little that a righteous man hath is better than the riches of many wicked. (17) For the arms of the wicked shall be broken: but the Lord upholdeth the righteous. (18) The Lord knoweth the days of the upright: and their inheritance shall be for ever. (19) They shall not be ashamed in the evil time: and in the days of famine they shall be satisfied. (20) But the wicked shall perish, and the enemies of the Lord shall be as the fat of lambs: they shall consume; into smoke shall they consume away. (21) The wicked borroweth, and payeth not again: but the righteous sheweth mercy, and giveth. (22) For such as be blessed of him shall inherit the earth; and they that be cursed of him shall be cut off. (23) The steps of a good man are ordered by the Lord: and he delighteth in his way. (24) Though he fall, he shall not be utterly cast down: for the Lord upholdeth him with his hand. (25) I have been young, and now am old; yet have I not seen the righteous forsaken, nor his seed begging bread. (26) He is ever merciful, and lendeth; and his seed is blessed. (27) Depart from evil, and do good; and dwell for evermore. (28) For the Lord loveth judgment, and forsaketh not his saints; they are preserved for ever: but the seed of the wicked shall be cut off. (29) The righteous shall inherit the land, and dwell therein for ever. (30) The mouth of the righteous speaketh wisdom, and his tongue talketh of judgment. (31) The law of his God is in his heart; none of his steps shall slide. (32) The wicked watcheth the righteous, and seeketh to slay him. (33) The Lord will not leave him in his hand, nor condemn him when he is judged. (34) Wait on the Lord, and keep his way, and he shall exalt thee to inherit the land: when the wicked are cut off, thou shalt see it. (35) I have seen the wicked in great power, and spreading himself like a green bay tree. (36) Yet he passed away, and, lo, he was not: yea, I sought him, but he could not be found. (37) Mark the perfect man, and behold the upright: for the end of that man is peace. (38) But the transgressors shall be destroyed together: the end of the wicked shall be cut off. (39) But the salvation of the righteous is of the Lord: he is their strength in the time of trouble. (40) And the Lord shall help them, and deliver them: he shall deliver them from the wicked, and save them, because they trust in him.*

If someone is strongly working against you in addition to these actions, obtain a glass candle of Saint Michael the Archangel. Dress the wick and the top of the candle with Send Back Evil Oil. Pray to St. Michael that the sun upon his sword and the force of his whip turn all work against you back to the one who has sent it, and that he bring swift retribution upon them. Burn this with the uncrossing candle.

The color of the uncrossing candle is not exceptionally important. Different writers recommend different colors. Black or white are often used.

St. Raphael

In 2015 I wrote a blog post about working with angels particularly fixated on impurity and sin, and how that created a greater need to be pure. I noted that in the system of work with which they are associated there is a story of a Rabbi spending forty days purifying himself so that he would be pure enough to receive the instructions on how to purify himself so that he would be pure enough to receive an angel. This is precisely what we're intending to work around. One of the conclusions I came up with at the time is that Saint Raphael the Archangel can magically help facilitate this.

The magic I provided in the blog post follows:

"As I'm sure you're aware Raphael is the archangel of the Sun. So let's look at how that plays into this.

1. The Sun provides direction and spiritual gravitas. The idea of impurity in a ritual sense or of sin is that of losing direction and wandering towards less beneficial ends. Invoking the Sun reflects the assertion of direction on your being.

2. The Sun is splendor and beauty, so Raphael makes you seem all shiny and clean.

3. Raphael provides healing. Healing spiritually relates to balancing imbalances, removing impurities, and making the incomplete complete. All of this fits with correcting the impacts of missing your mark.

4. The sun is the planetary force most similar to the Philosophers Stone, which has the power to correct and elevate. Kabbalistically Tifaret is the bridge which transmits the light into the material world and aspiration into the spiritual world.

5. And most importantly the Sun is the part of you that makes you awesome. The Sun within your being is the you that is YOU. It is the part of you for whom the concept of sin or impurity can't exist. It is the road to the Throne, which the Merkavah is all about, it's the light that leads you home back to the knowledge that you weren't impure, you were divine the whole time."

    The short take away is that the Sun provides direction and healing. These are the two things we need to apply to ourselves to achieve a state similar to "purity", so calling upon St. Raphael to facilitate this purpose is a viable solution.

For this, you will need a candle, a small vessel of either balsam or olive oil, and a small vessel of water.

Say this prayer:

Holy Father, Lord of Hosts, Most High God, Font of Mercy, send forth your healing through the gracious presence of your angel Raphael. Send your good angel upon me that I may be made whole. St. Raphael, pray for me and heal my

heart, my body and my soul, return me to a state of well-being, make me clean and whole. Bless this water that it may cleanse me, bless this oil that it may sanctify me. When I place them on my head, let it be your hands which wash away my sin, and which anoint me with grace. Amen.

Pour the water over the crown of your head. Anoint your forehead moving up to your hair line with the oil; press your hand with the oil on it on the crown of your head.

Mary

The Blessed Virgin Mary is the Mother of mankind and the Mother of Mercy. She has experienced sorrows beyond those of the average person and so she stands with us. She rules the legions of heaven and hell and thus has the power to command them in our favor and to aid us in our work with them. She is an ally in soothing and elevating the dead. She is a mother who will watch over us and ease our suffering and facilitate our success. Pointing me to Marianism has been one of the very powerful things my ancestors have done for me in my work with them. We do not need a great deal of ritual pomp and circumstance to turn to Mary. We can call upon her for many elements of this work. For the moment, we will call upon her to help make us ready.

Pray

Hail Mary, full of grace, the Lord is with you,
Blessed are you among women
and blessed is the fruit of your womb, Jesus
Holy Mary, Mother of God, pray for us sinners,
now and at the hour of our death
Amen
Mother of Mercy,
pour out your mercy upon all those who suffer
Especially pour out your mercy upon my ancestors,

soothe and elevate their spirits
Pour out your mercy upon my family and friends
Pour out your mercy upon those who bring me vexation,
that they too may learn mercy
Pour out your mercy upon me,
that I may have a merciful heart
Make me whole and well
that I may be successful in my endeavors
Bring good spirits and angels to me
that they may help me do wonderful things
Strengthen the dead that they may help me in this work
Amen.

Anointing

We talked about purification as being partially an act which creates tension and dynamism. The point of that tension or dynamism is to create a certain spiritual fire. This fire helps open us to experience – to be able to see and interact; with the spirits. It also gives us the force and authority to command. Engaging in regimens of spiritual work and development can cultivate this over time. The preparations from a grimoire can create a short-term cultivation as well.

If looking to engage in this work without those preparations, steps can be taken to invoke grace and spiritual fire. One simple idea is anointing. In Biblical stories and religious parlance, anointing goes along with the concept of receiving this sort of spiritual presence and power. A proper anointing oil can help open up awareness and stir an indwelling of spiritual fire, but generally in a temporary fashion and not with the same potency. Similarly, there are teas, salves, and incenses that can be used for these purposes and may have more potency, depending upon what is in them. If you are making your own oil, make sure to speak to the spirits of the components to awaken them, remind them of their power, and tell them what you want them to do. If you have purchased an oil, this is a good step too. If considering teas, salves or incenses, be careful to obtain them from reputable well-educated manufacturers.

Oils to consider using include Crown of Success, Abramelin, High John the Conqueror, and King Solomon Wisdom.

When using these oils place a bit on the tips of your fingers and anoint your forehead between the brows. Move up across each brow and place a dot in the center of the head. You might also anoint the crown of the head by placing the hand upon it or both hands as if conferring a blessing. The anointing should be done with a prayer to call upon the potency conferred by the oil.

The Holy Spirit

"This is the mystery of Pentecost: The Holy Spirit illuminates the human spirit and, by revealing Christ Crucified and Risen, indicates the way to become more like him, that is, to be 'the image and instrument of the love which flows from Christ.'"
(Pope Benedict XVI, June 4, 2006)

In Christian tradition, the visitation of the Holy Spirit at Pentecost fulfilled Christ's promise of the wonders that would be worked by his followers. This gave them the power to speak such that all listening could understand them and to heal the sick and command spirits. The apostolic power passed through the episcopate is the fullness of the priesthood achieved through this indwelling of the Holy Spirit. This form of initiation is a way of activating the spiritual charism that aids in this form of spirit work.

For those not ordained to the priesthood or consecrated to the episcopate, the visitation of the Holy Spirit can still be achieved as a means of tapping into divine grace and the spiritual fire used to see and command spirits. Before working, take time to sit in solitude, praying for the entry of the Holy Spirit. Repetitive prayer to enflame yourself in the fire of the spirit is the goal.

Here are some prayers to engage the Holy Spirit.

Breathe into me, Holy Spirit, that my thoughts may all be holy. Move in me, Holy Spirit, that my work, too, may be holy. Attract my heart, Holy Spirit, that I may love only what is holy. Strengthen me, Holy Spirit, that I may defend all that is holy. Protect me, Holy Spirit, that I may always be holy. Amen

O King of glory,
send us the Promise of the Father,
the Spirit of Truth.
May the Counselor
Who proceeds from You
enlighten us
and infuse all truth in us,
as You have promised.
Amen.

Come, Holy Spirit,
fill the hearts of your faithful,
and enkindle in us the fire of your love.
Send forth your Spirit and we shall be created,
and you shall renew the face of the earth.
Amen.

Hesychasm

In the Orthodox Christian Church there is a tradition of mystical prayer called Hesychasm. The name refers to silence. To really address the nature of the prayer, we would need a whole book in itself. I encourage people to explore writings on this prayer method if they feel called to deeper engagement.

The essential considerations of the prayer are ones of juxtaposition, and the goal is a state of prayer that draws an indwelling of divine light into the heart. Everything we have said about creating spiritual fire is reflected in those concepts. The Hesychast is aware of the body, but centered on the spirit. They speak a prayer, but do so in silence. They fix upon the heart, while focused upon the divine.

The prayer specifically calls upon the name of Jesus because it recognizes Jesus as God dwelling in the human condition, God in a state of bodily presence, and thus it calls to mind that the mystic may achieve a state of embodiedness which connects to the divine. The mystic looks to the heart to focus the prayer into the heart, so the presence of the prayer draws the divine light into the heart itself.

The prayer itself is simple:

Lord Jesus Christ, Son of God, have mercy on me, a sinner

The prayer should be prayed while seated in a secluded space, preferably one in which the senses are mitigated, a closet or a darkened room. The head and shoulders should be bowed so that the eyes gaze upon the chest focused on the heart. The prayer is bodily and so it should be matched to the rhythms of the body, first with the breath, but then potentially with the heart. As you breathe in, pray the first half of the prayer; as you breathe out, pray the second half of the prayer. The estimation is that a session of the prayer should last roughly twenty to thirty minutes with the prayer being said one hundred times. The prayer is said in silence; it is repeated in the mind and heart. The goal in praying this way is to draw the light of divine glory and perceive the aurora of this light as it inhabits the heart, or to come into a silent space drawn away from all else and perceive unity with Christ as he and the mystic indwell the heart.

Khernips

The khernips is part of our sine qua non of preparation. Khernips means to purify; it refers to the lustral water with which we purify ourselves before entering the temple space, as well as that with which we purify the temple space itself. When engaging in ritual we will make the khernips separately for each of these two purposes. The khernips removes miasma or pollution. The idea of miasma is that we are exposed to things which make us feel unclean or guilty or preoccupied. The khernips allows us to remove that sense of uncleanliness before beginning.

The khernips is traditionally made with running water because it represents the power of the goddesses who inhabit running water. Rain water or spring water are options, these can be mixed with tap water. The water is mixed with cleansing herbs and is empowered by having a smoldering bit of wood, or of rope, or a smoldering herb bundle dropped into the water as the magician says "kherniptosai." (pronounced: zer-nip-TOS-aye-ee)

Before entering the ritual space, strip down, take the bowl of water and the herbs, light the herbs and toss them into the bowl saying "kherniptosai." If you can pour water over your hands from the bowl, do so. Otherwise reach into the bowl, wash your hands with the water. Wash your face, under arms, genitals and feet. Once this is done then you can put on your ritual attire and enter the space.

Recap

We have presented several options for preparing yourself. The break-down is to prepare mental your state, to prepare your skill set, to engage your spiritual readiness and to make sure you are mentally prepared for what will happen.

We can't make you mentally prepared for what will happen. You have to figure that part out. We've provided some methods for preparing mental state and mental acuity; these might help with being prepared for what happens as well. There may be other methods you can use with these, or in lieu of these as well.

We did not give a lot of skill advice because you don't need to prep a lot of skills. Just being aware enough to have the experience is sufficient for now. A little experimentation with what was provided to develop occult senses will help you if you have not already done work for those efforts. The environment, the ritual, the incense, and similar sorts of materials can help with that as well.

As for spiritual preparedness, you have to judge what is necessary for you. Let your angel guide you on this. The Khernips should be the base line cleansing that is done in all cases. The uncrossing, the purification bath, the prayer to St. Raphael, and the prayer to Mary are options for cleansing. Mix and match as you see fit or use other methods. For empowerment, we have provided the bath for empowerment, the options for abstinence, the anointing, the prayer to the Holy Spirit and the Hesychastic prayer. Work with your Holy Guardian Angel can also facilitate this. Again, some effort at creating that spiritual fire is necessary, but you can determine which ones work for you and which ones are sufficient for you. We've given options; you need to do something, but you can sort out what works for you.

For a lot of grimoires, you're looking at about a nine-day purification period. Methods given here could reasonably be done in a day. The expectation is, if you've done no magic before, you could assemble the tools for this while doing these preparations and in about three to seven days be ready to try something. So with that, let's move on to the tools.

Luminarium

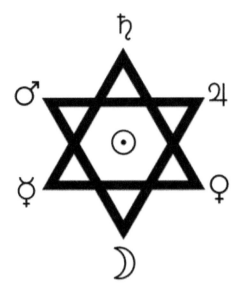

Luminarium

Tools and Space

Before you begin, you will need to obtain a small number of tools. You will also need to select a working space. The instructions below will describe the tools and any special considerations regarding preparing them. In most cases, the tools will need to be consecrated by sprinkling them with Holy Water and praying over them. If no specific instructions are given the prayer may be your own, or an appropriate Psalm may be selected. Nothing more complex is typically needed.

The space will need to be selected, cleaned and consecrated. Instructions for doing so are provided. The preparation of the space the first time will take one day prior to your work. Gathering and preparing the tools should not be difficult. Most will be obtainable at a local department store or grocery store if they are not already available in your home.

Tools

The work we will do will not be as tool intensive as many systems of spirit magic. The essential tools are thus:

Altar
Scrying Bowl
Khernips Bowl (2)
Cork or Rope or Bundle of Herbs
Holy Water
Lamp
Seal for the Holy Guardian Angel
Seal for the Spirit
Anointing Oil
Wand
Libations
Red Cloth
Grape Wood/Vine
Magnet
Silver Coin

Pebble
Seal of Solomon
Ring (Optional)
Ritual Attire
Candles
Incense Burner
Stones
Offering Bowl (2)

This might look like a lot, but you don't need six different knives, five swords, ten seals, virgin spun thread, and the various other things accreted to the grimoire work by the later grimoires. Most of these will be simple to collect and simple to prepare.

Altar (2)

You will need two altars. One will be a permanent altar for your ancestor shrine. This can be a shelf, or rack or table. It should be able to be placed up against a wall. If it is a cabinet or trunk which can hold your other supplies, all the better. The second altar will be for the actual conjurations. This should be a small table; it can be temporary and should fit in the space in front of your ancestor shrine.

We will give the details of your ancestor altar when discussing work with the ancestors. One of the offering bowls will go with the ancestor altar.

Scrying Bowl

The scrying bowl can be any simple shallow bowl. It does not need to be anything special. If you choose, you can paint this incantation on the bowl, but it is not necessary:

Atzam, Tzoalakoum, Geamai, Satzyne, Kalesaines, Ton, Tapesmas, Taphydou, Elylpe, Syltan, Gialoti, Mpalontzem, Thara, Pakhakhesesan, Sylbakhama, Mousamoukhana, Araga,

Rhasai, Rhagana, Obras, Ouboragoras, Tzoupa, Biapophkha, Tambalakhakem, Parakhematzoum, Tou, Itana, Baphoutia, Pakhakhe, Tanretokous, Nastratie, Parakhematzoum, Tou, Itana, Baphoutia, Pakhakhe, Tanretokous, Nastratie, Pakhakhyelea, Tybalotze, Enkaika, Parpara, Oumebras, Khematzoum

If you paint the incantation on the bowl it should either be in a non-water-soluble paint or sealed with a waterproof clear coat.

Khernips Bowl (2); Cork or Rope or Bundle of Herbs; Spring Water

You will need one Khernips for cleansing yourself before you enter your space and one for beginning the ritual. Any bowl large enough for you to wash your hands in will do for the one outside of the temple; a smaller bowl is fine for the one in the ritual. You can use hyssop, juniper, sage, rose or some other leaves or flowers which are associated with purification or sanctity. You can bundle the herbs to light and toss in, or you can have herbs in the water and then light a bit of string or cork or wood to activate it.

Holy Water

Holy Water will be used in consecrating tools. You should asperge any tool you use with Holy Water. You will also use it to sprinkle yourself and your space. You can obtain Holy Water at most Catholic Churches. Many occult shops and botanicas will sell it as well as Catholic supply shops. Often cities will have small grocery stores or candle shops which cater to traditional communities which are heavily Catholic and will have Holy Water.

The basic formula for making Holy Water is to consecrate or exorcise salt, exorcise water, and then combine them with a prayer for the salt to complete the exorcism and for God to sanctify the combination of the two. You need to have received the sacrament of Holy Orders to make Holy Water. We will present a method for making Holy Water for those who have received Orders, and we will present a method for requesting that an angel prepare salt and water for you if you have not received Orders. Technically the latter will not be Holy Water but should be functional enough. If you purchase Holy Water you can produce more Holy Water by mixing existing Holy Water with regular water so long as more than half the mixture was originally Holy Water.

Making Holy Water

Obtain a bowl of salt and a bowl of water, preferably from a clean natural source.

Place your right hand over the salt and say this prayer making the sign of the cross:

Our help is in the name of the Lord, who made heaven and earth. O salt, creature of God, I exorcise you by the living God, by the true God, by the holy God, by the God who ordered you to be poured into the water by Elisha the Prophet so that its life-giving powers might be restored. I exorcise you so that you may become a means of salvation for believers, that you may bring health of soul and body to all who make use of you, arid that you may put to flight and drive away from the places where you are sprinkled every apparition, villainy, and turn of devilish deceit, and every unclean spirit, adjured by Him Who will come to judge the living and the dead and the world by fire. Amen.

Place your right hand over the water and say this prayer making the sign of the cross:

O water, creature of God, I exorcise you in the name of God the Father almighty, and in the name of Jesus Christ His Son, our Lord, and in the power of the Holy Spirit. I exorcise you so that you may put to flight all the power of the Enemy, and be able to root out and supplant that Enemy with his apostate angels: through the power of our Lord Jesus Christ, Who will come to judge the living and the dead and the world by fire. Amen.

Combine the salt and water, pouring the salt into the water in the shape of a cross saying this prayer:

May this salt and water be mixed together; in the name of the Father, and of the Son, and of the Holy Spirit. Amen

Breathe upon the water and make the sign of the cross over the water blessing it with this prayer:

Blessed are you, Lord, Almighty God, who deigned to bless us in Christ, the living water of our salvation, and to reform us interiorly, grant that we who are fortified by the sprinkling of or use of this water, the youth of the spirit being renewed by the power of the Holy Spirit, may walk always in newness of life.

Angel Water

Obtain a bowl of salt, and a bowl of water, preferably from a clean natural source.

Pray

Holy Father, Lord of Hosts, Most High God, Font of Mercy, send forth your likeness through the gracious presence of your angel Michael. Send your good angel upon me that he may bless this water on my behalf, that I may use it in all good works.

Hold up the salt

St. Michael, by your scourge and the light of your sword cast out all iniquity from this salt, let any falsehood and unclean forces fly therefrom.

Hold up the water

St. Michael, by your scourge and the light of your sword cast out all iniquity from this water, let any falsehood and unclean forces fly therefrom.

Pour the salt into the water in the shape of a cross, pray:

St. Michael, let this salt mix with this water in the name of the Father the Son and the Holy Spirit. Amen.

Hold up the water and pray:

St. Michael, bless and sanctify this water, sanctify my prayer and pray now with me.

Blessed are you, Lord, Almighty God, who deigned to bless us in Christ, the living water of our salvation, and to reform us interiorly, grant that we who are fortified by the sprinkling of or use of this water, the youth of the spirit being renewed by the power of the Holy Spirit, may walk always in newness of life.

Holy Water should not be used in the scrying bowl, as an offering, or as the khernips water. A little may be sprinkled into a ritual bath, otherwise, use it for consecrations and blessings.

Lamp, Seal for the Holy Guardian Angel

The lamp should be an oil lamp, like a hurricane lamp,

or some lamp with an enclosed vessel for oil, a wick which may be wound up and down and a glass encasement for the wick. The lamp will be placed upon the altar during conjurations. It will be consecrated to your Holy Guardian Angel during the conjuration. You may paint a seal for your angel or his name on the lamp, or you may place the seal and name beneath the lamp when using it. You may use regular lamp oil or you may scent the oil with frankincense or Abramelin or an appropriate temple oil. Do not scent the lamp oil with scents for the spirits being conjured. If placing a seal for the angel beneath the lamp, it may be on paper or parchment, or on a wooden, clay or metal disk. Any such seal should be provided by your angel. If you do not have a seal it is not necessary to place one there.

Seal for the Spirit

Seals for any spirits being conjured may be drawn on paper or parchment and placed beneath the scrying bowl. They should be consecrated with holy water, they may be dotted with a five spot of appropriate oil (one spot in the center and one at each corner). The seal can be written in regular ink, or an appropriate magical ink.

Anointing Oil

Anointing oil is optional. You can use an anointing oil such as one of the ones we mentioned in the preparation section, or you can anoint with an oil appropriate to the spirit being conjured. Seals and candles may also be dressed with oil appropriate to the spirit being conjured. When dressing a candle, if you are dressing the candle for the spirit being conjured, rub the oil clockwise and towards you. If you are dressing the candle for a spell which will be worked with the spirit, then rub the oil clockwise and towards you (wick to base) if you are drawing something in, or counter-clockwise and away (base to wick) if pushing something away. Candles used as part of the standard altar set up are for the spirit; candles used in a particular spell or spirit action are for that working. You will need oil for scrying. This may be the anointing oil or simply olive oil.

Wand

The wand will not be a particularly operant tool. In the ancient world the wand was a symbol of power and of status as a magician. The status as a magician implies the authority and power to command spirits. The wand is here for this purpose. It may be any appropriate wooden rod roughly seven to twelve inches in length. Nut bearing trees which have not borne nuts are traditional. Oak is an opportune choice for its regency. Otherwise, grapewood, rosewood, or laurel would have significant power.

Libations

Your ancestors will inform you of the appropriate libation to give them. Whiskey, rum, or beer are common. For other spirits we will use wine. Any red wine may be used. The libations for the ancestors will be poured into the cup on their altar; other spirits will receive libations into the offering cup or bowl on the main altar.

Red Cloth

The red cloth may be of any type and should be sufficient to cover the crown of the head. It may cover further, from the hairline back, if desired, so long as it covers at least the crown. It should be able to be placed upon the head and remain there on its own. This can be done with bobby pins, or by sewing the covering to fit like a cap or head dressing. A cloth which can be wrapped over the head like a turban may be used as well.

Grape Wood/Vine

A dry piece of grape wood or vine of size to fit in the scrying bowl.

Magnet

A small natural magnet.

Silver Coin

A silver bearing coin is preferred but any silver colored coin may be used.

Pebble

The pebble should have the number 3663 painted thereon.

Seal of Solomon

The magician does not need the Great Seal of Solomon or any seal for binding spirits. If the magician wishes to conjure an aerial spirit to serve beneath the archangel for some material purpose, the magician should possess the planetary seal for commanding spirits of that order. The seal may be drawn on paper, parchment or vellum in regular ink, or an appropriate magical ink. It should be consecrated with holy water, censed, and oiled before-hand, with the Psalm prayed over it.

Ring (Optional)

If the magician has acquired a Ring of Solomon, or a general magical ring associated with the angels and the command of spirits he should wear it. If he has not, it is not necessary. A rosary, a miraculous medal, or some other tool of divine presence may be worn along with or in lieu of the ring, but is not mandatory.

Ritual Attire

The magician may wear ritual attire as deemed appropriate. You should not work in the nude as you will be working with your ancestors. Do not wear the clothes that you were wearing during the day prior to the work. You may wear clean fresh clothes of a normal variety, or a ritual robe. In all cases remove whatever you were wearing before, clean yourself, and put on your ritual clothing.

Candles

You will use a number of candles for your ancestor altar. Votive candles or tea lights are appropriate for this. The color for these is unimportant but it is good for them to be uniform. White or a natural wax color are well suited to this, or some particular color for your family.

For particular workings you might use a variety of candles. Votives, chime candles, table candles, glass-encased candles, and taper candles all have their appropriate uses. You will need these in a variety of colors.

For the main altar you will need four candles, all of one color. Generally, they will be white, but you may use a color appropriate to the angel being conjured, should you so choose.

Your candles may be blessed by sprinkling with holy water while using the following prayers:

O almighty, everlasting God, who didst command the purest oil to be prepared by Thy servant Moses to keep lamps continually before Thee; graciously pour forth the grace of Thy blessing + upon these candles; they may so afford external light, that by Thy gift the light of Thy Spirit may not fail interiorly in our minds. In the name of the Father, the Son, and the Holy Spirit, amen.

Luminarium

Psalm 150 *(1) Praise ye the Lord. Praise God in his sanctuary: praise him in the firmament of his power. (2) Praise him for his mighty acts: praise him according to his excellent greatness. (3) Praise him with the sound of the trumpet: praise him with the psaltery and harp. (4) Praise him with the timbrel and dance: praise him with stringed instruments and organs. (5) Praise him upon the loud cymbals: praise him upon the high sounding cymbals. (6) Let every thing that hath breath praise the Lord. Praise ye the Lord.*

I bless thee in the Name of the Father. O Holy, Holy Lord, God, Heaven and Earth are full of Thy Glory before Whose face there is a bright shining light forever; bless now, O Lord, I beseech Thee, these creatures of light which Thou hast given for the Kindly use of man that they, by Thee being sanctified, may not be put out or extinguished by the power, malice, or filthy darkness of the Adversary, but may shine forth brightly and lend their assistance to this my Work, through Jesus Christ our Lord. Amen.

Candles consecrated to a particular angel may be blessed using the same prayers and Holy Water. Additionally, the angel's name and seal may be carved into the candle and the appropriate Orphic hymn may be added to the prayers.

In consideration of candle colors, we will use the color associated with the planet for candles dedicated to the angel of a given planet.

Saturn – Black
Jupiter – Blue
Mars – Red
Sol – Yellow or Gold
Venus – Green
Mercury – Orange

Luna – Silver or White

For spells and practical purposes you may use the same color scheme, or use more intuitive ones – pink for affection, red for passion, green for money, as examples. For more comprehensive treatment of this obtain *The Master Book of Candleburning* by Henri Gamache.

Incense Burner

Preferably a charcoal incense burner should be used. Any suitable burner for the type of incense you are using is fine. You may need a heat-proof layer to place under your burner.

Incense and Herbs

Incenses and herbs will be prepared and stored before their use. Particular preparations of incense may be made to aid in work with particular sorts of spirits. We will simply provide the core incense for the given orders of spirits. Herbs may be used in addition to the incense for particular workings.

In all cases when you obtain the incense or herb and before its use, wake it up by speaking to it. Remind it of its nature and power. Talk with it about how it will be used. Ask it for its aid.

For both incense and herbs use this prayer:

You were sown by Kronos, you were conceived by Hera, / you were maintained by Ammon, you were given birth by Isis, you were nourished by Zeus the god of rain, you were given growth by Helios and dew. You [are] the dew of all the gods, you [are] the heart of Hermes, you are the seed of the primordial gods, you are the eye / of Helios, You are the light of Selene, you are the zeal of Osiris, you are the beauty and the glory of Ouranos, you are the soul of Osiris' daimon which revels in every place, you are the spirit of Ammon. As you have exalted Osiris, so / exalt yourself and rise just as Helios rises each day. Your size is equal to the zenith of Helios, your roots come from the depths, but your powers are in the heart of Hermes, your fibers are the bones of Mnevis, and your / flowers are the eye of Horus, your seed is Pan's seed. I am washing you in resin as I also wash the gods even [as I do this] for my own health. You also be cleaned by prayer and give us power as Ares and Athena do. I am Hermes. I am acquiring you with Good / Fortune and Good Daimon both at a propitious hour and on a propitious day that is effective for all things.

For incenses use the appropriate Orphic hymn along with this prayer:

The God of Abraham, God of Isaac, God of Jacob, bless here these spice that they may fill up the power and virtue of their odors; so that neither the enemy, nor any false imagination, may be able to enter into them: through our Lord Jesus Christ, in the Name of the Father, the Son and the Holy Spirit, Amen.

Generally, your incenses will be as follows:

Saturn – traditionally Sulfur, but Black Pepper or Myrrh may be used because of the dangers of Sulfur
Jupiter – Saffron or Cedar
Mars – Pepper or tobacco
Sol – Red Sandalwood or Frankincense
Venus – Costus or Rose
Mercury – Gum Arabic or Balsam
Luna – Agar Wood or Jasmine or Dittany of Crete

Stones

You may wish to have colored stones, or particular sorts of stones, and magnets for particular magical endeavors. These will also be useful in consecrating talismans.

Offering Bowl (2)

You will need a bowl or cup into which to pour libations. One of these will go upon your ancestor altar and one upon the main altar.

Space

The space for this ritual will be slightly different from the typical space for ceremonial working. We won't be building up a big temple with pillars and steps and banners; we don't need black and white tiles. We don't need a mat with a floor circle, or a wooden floor to scratch, or a floor on which we can write with chalk. We're working in a bit more of a folk context. We're working like cunning folk, so we're working in a space in which we reside. We're working with angels and we have spirits to help protect us, so we don't need circles and names of God on the floor – but we do need a sanctified space suited to the spirits.

The main part of the space will be the shrine for the ancestors. The ancestors are the anchor. They guide and protect us; they empower us and they humanize the work to make manifestations that are suited to our human needs. The ancestor shrine will be a permanent set-up, which we will talk about when we discuss the ancestors. It should be in a safe spot in your home with space in front of it where you can work. It should set against a wall so it won't get knocked over and things won't fall off. You will need room in front of the ancestor shrine where you can place a small table to use as an altar and a chair at which you can sit. The table and the chair do not need to be there permanently but should be there when you consecrate the space. You won't need to do this consecration each time you work, but you should do it periodically when not doing other work.

Cleansing and Consecrating the Space

Before you begin, wash the shrine, the table, the chair, and the tools. Scrub the floor. You can do this using Florida water, or ask your ancestors if there is a mixture they prefer. I usually use some Florida water, 90% Isopropyl Alcohol, Lilet Blanc, and Old Spice blended together. Scrub everything thoroughly while praying however you are moved to pray. Be happy in the service you are doing for your spirits. Wipe everything down afterwards with Holy Water while praying Hail Marys.

Now, light a candle. Pray quietly from your heart for your Angel and for God to bless the space.

Perform service at your ancestor shrine. We will go over how to do this when we talk about the ancestors.

Light some incense, circle the space with the incense and blow the smoke over the shrine, the altar and the tools while praying the Psalm.

Psalm 47 *(1) O clap your hands, all ye people; shout unto God with the voice of triumph. (2) For the Lord most high is terrible; he is a great King over all the earth. (3) He shall subdue the people under us, and the nations under our feet. (4) He shall choose our inheritance for us, the excellency of Jacob whom he loved. Selah. (5) God is gone up with a shout, the Lord with the sound of a trumpet. (6) Sing praises to God, sing praises: sing praises unto our King, sing praises. (7) For God is the King of all the earth: sing ye praises with understanding. (8) God reigneth over the heathen: God sitteth upon the throne of his holiness. (9) The princes of the people are gathered together, even the people of the God of Abraham: for the shields of the earth belong unto God: he is greatly exalted.*

Sprinkle the quarters with Holy Water while saying this prayer:

Divine Light, Immovable Mover, Limitlessness who is wholly present and wholly active in every place created and uncreated; hearken to this earnest prayer, and be the sanctity of this dwelling. Let no vileness of hostile powers prevail here, let no falsehood deter those herein, but by the working of the Holy Guardian Angel may a faultless service always be

rendered to the Work in this place, and a holy liberty abound; through the light of the Lord of Hosts.

Leave the incense on the altar and let the candles burn. Let the space alone for it can sanctify for a day. Then return to it for your work after this is all done.

Luminarium

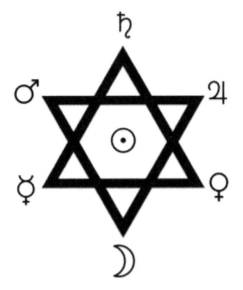

Relationships

A person can walk into a magic shop, buy a spell, a few supplies, and try a spell. Maybe it works, maybe it doesn't. This one-off does not make them a magician or a sorcerer. Building a practice which leads to more successful magic makes one a sorcerer or a magician. Central to that is a consistent relationship with the spirits with whom you will work. If you have gathered your tools and done your preparations you can hop right in and do the rituals as presented in this book. If you have the opportunity beforehand, engaging in some relationship building will help. If you need to get started right away due to some particular need, go for it. You can begin building relationships afterwards as you continue to work.

We are going to make recommendations for practices for building a relationship with Hekate, your ancestors, the elementals, your Guardian Angel, and the angels of the planets.

Hekate

Hekate is a central force in magic and an important ally to have. Like any god she, can be approached with hymns and prayers and offerings, but the means by which she wishes you to approach her may be peculiar to the relationship she has in mind. You could recite her Orphic Hymn each night and pray to be visited in dreams. You could go to the crossroads and make offerings while praying her hymn.

Each month there is a night on which offerings are made to her called the Deipnon. For this prepare an offering of food. Traditionally, bread, sweet cakes, honey, eggs, fish, leeks or onions are foods likely to be included. I will often use a pita or flat bread as the base, drizzle it with honey, and then place the other foods on top of it. This should be left at a crossroads or at the edge of one's property. Once you set the offering down turn and do not look back. The Deipnon occurs on the night of the Dark Moon, or the night before the first sliver of the New Moon appears. On the Deipnon, Hekate leads the restless dead; the food pacifies them. Old offerings left on shrines or food or offerings which have fallen to the floor may be added to Hekate's Deipnon offering.

Ancestors

The ancestors are a central part of what we will be doing magically. They may not seem to be the center of the work when we look at the ritual, but they help sanctify the space, and guide the spirit work. They provide the leverage and power needed to engage this work without necessarily going through copious preparations. Because of this our ritual set up will be done in front of the ancestor shrine.

Before setting up your shrine you should begin by talking to your ancestors. If you do not have an ancestor practice it is fairly easy to start. First, take a bath to relax yourself. Dress comfortably. Dim the lights in your house, and sit down at your table, having cleaned the table and neatened up the room. Light a candle, burn a little incense – frankincense or myrrh; or a scent that an ancestor you're close to liked. If there was a cologne that an ancestor you're close to wore, wear that. Set a plate of food for yourself and another for your ancestors. Pour them a glass of water. Begin talking. Let them know you want them to come speak with you and sit with you. Tell them about your day, about things going on in your life, and in the lives of your family members. Then sit in silence and listen. Enjoy the comfort of their presence. When you're done, thank them for their time. Clean up your plate, but leave their plate, water, and candle.

Now that you've begun talking with them, set up your shrine. You will need a cup or bowl for offerings, and a burner for incense. I often offer a scented candle. You might place some memento mori on the altar. Pictures of your ancestors, or items belonging to them, can go there. You'll need a cup for water along with the offering cup. I use small glass votive jars for my candles. You could also use glass jars with tea lights.

For each specific ancestor you wish to personally call upon and acknowledge, set a jar. These should be ancestors you knew in life, or ones that have some importance either in terms of your lineage or in terms of standing out in some meaningful way. Use a single candle to represent all of your not-named blood ancestors and another for all those not related by blood. (Ancestors can be ideological, or inspirational as well as lineal.) In the front of the altar place two coins for the ferryman.

Your ritual for opening your ancestor altar will be somewhat personal. Here are the essential points.
1. Knock three times to wake the dead
2. Call upon the ferryman (whoever keeps the dead or grants access to them) while touching his coins. Ask him to bring your ancestors and your allies to partake of these offerings, and let him know that he may partake as well for his service.
3. Call upon the gods of the underworld, or whatever powers oversee the dead. Ask that they strengthen your dead and come forth with them to partake of the offerings.
4. Light the incense and make a statement about sweetening the world, or imparting gifts associated with the particular incense.
5. Light the candles, stating for whom each candle is lit
6. Welcome the dead and thank them for aid they have previously given. Talk with them about your needs. Give them offerings in thanks for previous work, and offerings you're giving in anticipation of new work
7. If you're doing other magic with them, do it now. If you're just doing service at your ancestor altar, you're done. You can sit with them, you can talk with them, or you can thank them and bid them to enjoy their gifts. Leave their candles to burn.

In the space preparation when we talk about doing your ancestor service, this outline is that process. In the rituals coming up we will give the same instruction, to perform your ancestor service. Again, this is what you will do in that case.

The Elementals

The Elementals – the gnomes, sylphs, undines, and salamanders; are generally happy to work with humans. They recognize humans as reflecting the image of the creator, and in their love for the creator they seek to serve his reflection. Their reward is getting to stand with humankind and feel elevated in their prayers to the creator. If you choose to engage the elementals in your conjurations you will call upon them early so that they can stand with you through the conjuration. This way they will feel part of the process and be privy to your requests. They will stand with you while calling upon the angel, something they long to do. Since this is what they want there is less to do to build a relationship with the elementals, because the work itself will build a relationship. However, should you desire greater awareness of how they can help you, or should you wish to make contact to begin stirring their efforts in your favor, simply stand in the direction from which they arrive (gnomes – North, sylphs – East, undines – West, salamanders – South) and say their prayer. You can light a candle when you say the prayer and then meditate in their presence to learn from them, or say a psalm of praise and rejoicing with them so that they enjoy having stood with you in honor of the creator.

Here are their prayers:

Prayer of the Gnomes

Invisible King who has taken the earth as a support, and who has dug abysses in order to fill them with the omnipotence! Thou whose name makest the arches of the world tremble!

Thou who makest the seven metals circulate in the veins of stone; Monarch of seven luminaries! Rewarder of subterranean workmen! bring us to the desirable air and to the kingdom of light. We watch and work without respite. We seek and hope by the twelve stones of the Holy City, for the talismans which are buried by the magnetic nail which passes through the center of the earth. Lord! Lord! Lord! Have pity upon those who suffer! Enlarge our hearts! Let us be free and raise up our heads! Exalt us! O stability and movement! O Day invested by night! O Darkness veiled in light! O Master who never retainest the wages of thy workmen! O silvery whiteness! O Golden Splendor! O Crown of Diamonds, living and melodious! Thou who bearest the sky upon thy finger, like a ring of sapphire! Thou who hidest under the earth, in the kingdom of gems, the wonderful seed of stars! All hail! Reign; and be the Eternal Dispenser of riches, of which thou hast made us the guardians. Amen.

Prayer of the Sylphs

Spirit of light! Spirit of wisdom! whose breath gives and takes away again the forms of all things! Thou, in whose presence the life of being is a shadow which changes, and a vapor which passes away. Thou who ascendest the clouds and movest on the wing of the winds. When thou breathest forth, infinite spaces are peopled! When thou inhalest, all that comes from thee returns to thee! Endless movement in eternal stability, be thou eternally blest! We praise thee and bless thee in the changing empire of created light, of shadows, of reflections and of images; and we long unceasingly for thine immutable and imperishable light. Let the ray of thy intelligence and the heat of thy love penetrate even to us; then what is movable will become fixed; the shadow will become a body; the spirit of the air will become a soul; the dream will become a thought, and we shall no longer be borne away by the tempest, but shall hold the bridle of the winged steeds of the morning, and shall direct the course of the evening winds that we may fly into thy presence. O spirit of spirits! O eternal soul of souls! O imperishable breath of life! O creative inspiration. O mouth which inspires and respires the existence of all beings in the flux and reflux of thy eternal Word, which is the divine ocean of movement and of truth. Amen!

Prayer of the Undines

Terrible king of the sea! Thou who boldest the keys of the cataracts of heaven, and who enclosest the subterranean waters in the hollow places of the earth! King of the deluge and of rains, of springtime! Thou who openest the sources of streams and fountains! Thou who commandest the moisture (which is like the blood of the earth) to become the sap of plants! We adore and invoke thee! Speak to us, ye moving and changeable creatures! Speak to us in the great commotions of the sea, and we will tremble before thee. Speak to us also in the murmur of the limpid waters, and we will desire thy love. O immensity in which all the rivers of being lose themselves, which ever spring up anew in us! O ocean of infinite perfections! Height which beholdeth thee in the depth! Depth which breathes thee forth in the height! Bring us to the true life through intelligence and love! Lead us to immortality through sacrifice, in order that one day we may be found worthy to offer thee water, blood, and tears, for the remission of sins. Amen.

Prayer of the Salamanders

Immortal, eternal, ineffable and uncreated Father of all things I who are borne upon the incessantly rolling chariot of Worlds which are always turning; Ruler of the ethereal immensity where the throne of thy power is elevated; from whose height thy dread-inspiring eyes discover all things, and thy exquisite and sacred ears hear all; Listen to thy children whom thou hast loved from the beginning of the ages; for thy golden, great, and eternal majesty is resplendent above the world and the starry heavens. Thou art raised above them O sparkling fire! There thou dost illumine and support thyself by thine own splendor; and there comes forth from thine essence overflowing streams of light which nourish thine infinite spirit. That infinite spirit nourishes all things, and renders this inexhaustible treasure of substance always ready for the generation which fashions it and which receives in itself the forms with which thou hast impregnated it from the beginning. From this spirit those most holy kings who surround thy throne, and who compose thy court, derive their origin. O Father Universal! Only One! O Father of blessed mortals and immortals! Thou hast specially created powers who are marvelously like thine eternal thought and adorable essence. Thou hast established them superior to the angels who announce to the world thy wishes. Finally thou hast created us in the third rank in our elementary empire. There our continual employment is to praise thee and adore thy wishes. There we incessantly burn with the desire of possessing thee, O Father! O Mother! the most tender of all mothers! O admirable archetype of maternity and pure love! O Son, the flower of sons! O Form of all forms; soul, spirit, harmony and number of all things. Amen.

Daily Prayers

Many magicians both historical and modern have suggested reciting daily the conjurations of the archangels, even when the magician is not engaged in conjuring them. At the very least, it should be considered an activity to be done upon waking on days on which the magician intends to conjure. The conjurations are associated with the given day, so they conjure not just the archangel but the forces of the day itself. Along with this the magician should pray to his Guardian Angel to teach, guide and empower him in his work.

Here are two traditional prayers to the Guardian Angel

O angel of God, whom God hath appointed to be my guardian, enlighten and protect, direct and govern me. Amen

Angel of God, my guardian dear,
To whom His love commits me here,
Ever this day be at my side,
To light and guard, to teach and guide. Amen.

The Headless One

The magician may also consider using the Headless Invocation or the Stele of Jeu from the Greek Magical Papyri as a general exorcism to bind all spirits to obedience. Daily recitation can serve as an invocation to establish spiritual authority. Here is the version presented by S.L. MacGregor Mathers as the "Bornless Invocation":

Thee I invoke, the Bornless one.
Thee, that didst create the Earth and the Heavens:
Thee, that didst create the Night and the Day.
Thee, that didst create the Darkness and the Light.
Thou art Osorronophris:
Whom no man hath seen at any time.
Thou art Jabas:
Thou art Iapos:
Thou has distinguished between the just and the unjust.
Thou didst make the female and the male.
Thou didst produce the Seed and the Fruit.
Thou didst form Men to love one another, and to hate one another.

I am Mosheh Thy Prophet, unto Whom Thou didst commit Thy Mysteries, the Ceremonies of Israel.

Thou didst produce the Moist and the Dry, and that which norisheth all created life.

Hear Thou Me, for I am the Angel of Paphro Osorronophris; this is Thy True Name, handed down to the Prophets of Ishrael.

Hear Me: —

Ar: Thiao: Rheibet: Atheleberseth:
A: Blata: Abeu: Ebeu: Phi:
Thitasoe: Ib: Thiao.

Hear Me, and make all Spirits subject unto Me: so that every Spirit of the Firmament and of the Ether: upon the Earth and under the Earth: on Dry Land and in the Water: of Whirling Air, and of Rushing Fire: and every Spell and Scourge of God may be obedient unto Me.

I invoke Thee, the Terrible and Invisible God: Who dwellest in the Void Place of the Spirit.

Arogogorobrao: Sothou:
Modorio: Phalarthao: Doo: Ape, The
Bornless One:

Hear Me, and make all Spirits subject unto Me: so that every Spirit of the Firmament and of the Ether: upon the Earth and under the Earth: on Dry Land and in the Water: of Whirling Air, and of Rushing Fire: and every Spell and Scourge of God may be obedient unto Me.

Hear me: —

Roubriao: Mariodam: Balbnabaoth:
Assalonai: Aphniao: I: Thoteth:
Abrasar: Aeoou: Ischure,
Mighty and Bornless One!

Hear Me, and make all Spirits subject unto Me: so that every Spirit of the Firmament and of the Ether: upon the Earth and under the Earth: on Dry Land and in the Water: of Whirling Air, and of Rushing Fire: and every Spell and Scourge of God may be obedient unto Me.

I invoke Thee: —

Ma: Barraio: Ioel: Kotha:
Athorebalo: Abraoth:

Hear Me, and make all Spirits subject unto Me: so that every Spirit of the Firmament and of the Ether: upon the Earth and under the Earth: on Dry Land and in the Water: of Whirling Air, and of Rushing Fire: and every Spell and Scourge of God may be obedient unto Me.

Hear Me!

Aoth: Abaoth: Basum: Isak:
Sabaoth: Iao:

This is the Lord of the Gods:
This is the Lord of the Universe:
This is He Whom the Winds fear.

This is He, Who having made Voice by
His Commandment, is Lord of All Things;
King, Ruler and Helper

Hear Me, and make all Spirits subject unto Me: so that every Spirit of the Firmament and of the Ether: upon the Earth and under the Earth: on Dry Land and in the Water: of Whirling Air, and of Rushing Fire: and every Spell and Scourge of God may be obedient unto Me.

Hear Me: —

Ieou: Pur: Jou: Pur: Iaot: Iaeo: Ioou:
Abrasar: Sabriam: Do: Uu: Adonai: Ede: Edu:
Angelos ton Theon: Anlala Lai: Gaia: Ape:
Diathana Thorun.

I Am He! the Bornless Spirit! having sight in the Feet: Strong, and the Immortal Fire!

I am He! The Truth!

I Am He! Who hate the evil should be wrought in the World!
I am He, that lighteneth and thundereth.
I am He, from whom is the Shower of the Life of Earth:
I am He, whose mouth ever flameth:
I am He, the Begetter and Manifester unto the Light:
I am He, the Grace of the World:

THE HEART GIRT WITH A SERPENT is My Name!

Come Thou forth, and follow Me: and make all Spirits subject unto Me so that every Spirit of the Firmament, and of the Ether: upon the Earth and under the Earth: on Dry land, or in the Water: of whirling Air or of rushing Fire: and every Spell and Scourge of God, may be obedient unto Me!

Iao: Sabao:

— Such are the words —

A Prayer From Reginald Scot

Reginald Scot provides a similar prayer in his Discouerie of Witchcraft which invokes the Trinity, particularly Christ, by a slew of magical names to bind all spirits to obedience:

In the name of our Lord Jesus Christ the + Father + and the Son + and the Holy Ghost + Holy Trinity and Inseparable Unity, I call upon You, that You may be my salvation and defense, and the protection of my body and soul, and of all my goods through the virtue of Your Holy Cross, and through the virtue of Your passion, I beseech You O Lord Jesus Christ, by the merits of Your blessed mother Holy Mary, and of all Your saints, that You give me grace and divine power over all the wicked spirits, so as which of them soever I do call by name, they may come by and by from every coast, and accomplish my will, that they neither be hurtful or fearful unto me, but rather obedient and diligent about me. And through Your virtue straightly commanding them, let them fulfill my commands, Amen. Holy, holy, Lord God of Sabboth, which will come to judge the quick and the dead, You who are Alpha and Omega, first and last, King of kings and Lord of lords, Ioth, Aglanabrath, El, Abiel, Anathiel, Amazim, Sedomel, Gayes, Heli, Messias, Tolimi, Elias, Ischiros, Athanatos, Imas. By these Your holy names, and by all others I do call upon You, and beseech You O Lord Jesus Christ, by Your nativity and baptism, by thy cross and passion, by Your ascension, and by the coming of the Holy-Ghost, by the bitterness of Your soul when it departed from Your body, by Your five wounds, by the blood and water which went out of Your body, by Your virtue, by the sacrament which You gave Your disciples the day before You suffered, by the Holy trinity, and by the inseparable unity, by blessed Mary Your mother, by Your angels, archangels, prophets, patriarchs, and by all Your saints, and by all the sacraments which are made in Your honor, I do worship and beseech You, I bless and desire You, to accept these prayers, conjurations, and words of my mouth, which I will use. I require You O Lord Jesus Christ, that You give me Your virtue & power over all Your angels to draw them to me, to tie and bind them, & also to loose them, to gather them together before me, & to command them to do all that they can, and that by no means they contemn my voice, or the words of my mouth; but that they obey me and my sayings, and fear me. I beseech You by Your humanity, mercy and grace, and I require You Adonai, Amay, Horta, Vege dora, Mitai, Hel, Suranat, Ysion, Ysesy, and by all Your holy names, and by all Your holy he saints and she saints, by all Your angels and archangels, powers, dominions, and virtues, and by that name that Solomon did bind the devils, and shut them up, Elhrach, Ebanher, Agla, Goth, Ioth, Othie, Venoch, Nabrat, and by all Your holy names which are written in this book, and by the virtue of them all, that You enable me to congregate all Your spirits thrown down from heaven, that they may give me a true answer of all my demands, and that they satisfy all my requests, without the hurt of my body or soul, or any thing else that is mine, through our Lord Jesus Christ Your son, who lives and reigns with You in the unity of the Holy-Ghost, one God world without end.

Oh Father omnipotent, Oh wise Son, Oh Holy-Ghost, the searcher of hearts, oh you three in persons, one true godhead in substance, which did spare Adam and Eve in their sins; and Oh You Son, who died for their sins a most filthy death, sustaining it upon the Holy Cross; oh You most merciful, when I fly unto Your mercy, and beseech You by all the means I can, by these the holy names of Your Son; to wit, Alpha and Omega, and all of his other names, grant me Your virtue and power, that I may be able to cite before me, Your spirits which were thrown down from heaven, & that they may speak with me, & dispatch by & by without delay, & with a good will, & without the hurt of my body, soul, or goods, etc: as is contained in the book called Annulus Salomonis.

Oh great and eternal virtue of the highest, which through disposition, these being called to judgment, Vaicheon, Stimulamaton, Esphares, Tetragrammaton, Olioram, Cryon, Esytion, Existion, Eriona, Onela, Brasim, Noym, Messias, Soter, Emanuel, Sabboth, Adonai, I worship You, I invoke You, I implore You with all the strength of my mind, that by You, my present prayers, consecrations, and conjurations be hallowed: and wheresoever wicked spirits are called, in the virtue of Your names, they may come together from every coast, and diligently fulfill the will of me the exorcist. Fiat, fiat, fiat, Amen.

These prayers may be used each morning to stir the appropriate powers and to bring the magician into the orbits of the angels. We will also include the seven Orphic Hymns appropriate to this effort.

The seven conjurations we will use are as follows:

Sunday

Orphic Hymn

*Hear golden Titan, whose eternal eye
With broad survey, illumines all the sky.
Self-born, unwearied in diffusing light,
And to all eyes the mirror of delight:
Lord of the seasons, with your fiery car
And leaping coursers, beaming light from far:
With thy right hand the source of morning light,
And with thy left the father of the night.
Agile and vigorous, venerable Sun,
Fiery and bright around the heavens you run.
Foe to the wicked, but the good man's guide,
Over all his steps propitious you preside:
With various founding, golden lyre, 'tis mine
To fill the world with harmony divine.*

Luminarium

Father of ages, guide of prosperous deeds,
The world's commander, borne by lucid steeds,
Immortal Jove, all-searching, bearing light,
Source of existence, pure and fiery bright
Bearer of fruit, almighty lord of years,
Agile and warm, whom every power reveres.
Great eye of Nature and the starry skies,
Doomed with immortal flames to set and rise
Dispensing justice, lover of the stream,
The world's great despot, and over all supreme.
Faithful defender, and the eye of right,
Of steeds the ruler, and of life the light:
With founding whip four fiery steeds you guide,
When in the car of day you glorious ride.
Propitious on these mystic labors shine,
And bless thy suppliants with a life divine.

Conjuration

I conjure and confirm upon you, you strong and holy angels of God, in the name Adonai, Eheieh, Eheieh, Eya, which is he who was, and is, and is to come, Eye, Abray; and in the name Shaddai, Kadosh, Kadosh, sitting on high upon the Kerubim; and by the great name of God himself, strong and powerful, who is exalted above all the heavens; Eye, Saraye, who created the world, the heavens, the earth, the sea, and all that is in them, in the first day, and scaled them with his holy name Phaa; and by the name of the angels who rule in the fourth heaven, and serve before the most mighty Salamia, an angel great and honorable; and by the name of his star, which is Sol, and by his sign, and by the immense name of the living God, and by all the names aforesaid, I conjure you, Raphael, O great angel! who is chief ruler of this day; and by the name Adonai, the God of Israel, I conjure you, O Raphael! that you will labor for me, and fulfill all my petitions according to my will and desire in my cause and business!

<u>Luminarium</u>

Monday

Orphic Hymn

HEAR, Goddess queen, diffusing silver light,
Bull-horned and wandering through the gloom of Night.
With stars surrounded, and with circuit wide
Night's torch extending, through the heavens you ride:
Female and Male with borrowed rays you shine,
And now full orbed, now tending to decline.
Mother of ages, fruit-producing Moon,
Whose amber orb makes Night's reflected noon:
Lover of horses, splendid, queen of Night,
All-seeing power bedecked with starry light.
Lover of vigilance, the foe of strife,
In peace rejoicing, and a prudent life:
Fair lamp of Night, its ornament and friend,
Who gives to Nature's works their destined end.
Queen of the stars, all-wife Artemis hail!
Decked with a graceful robe and shining veil;
Come, blessed Goddess, prudent, starry, bright,
Come moonlit lamp with chaste and splendid light,
Shine on these sacred rites with prosperous rays,
And pleased accept thy suppliant's mystic praise.

Conjuration

I conjure and confirm upon you, strong and good angels, in the name Adonai, Adonai, Adonai, Adonai, Eheieh, Eheieh, Eheieh; Kadosh, Kadosh, Kadosh, Yehoiakim, Yehoiakim, Yah, Yah, strong Yah, who appeared in mount Sinai with the glorification of king Adonai, Shaddai, Tzavot, Anathay, Yah, Yah, Yah, Maranata, Abimelek, Jeia, who created the sea, and all lakes and waters, in the second day, which are above the heavens and in the earth, and scaled the sea in his high name, and gave it its bounds beyond which it cannot pass;

and by the names of the angels who rule in the first legion, and who serve Orphaniel, a great, precious, and honorable angel, and by the name of his star which is Luna, and by all the names aforesaid, I conjure thee, Gabriel, who art chief ruler of Monday, the second day, that for me you shall labor and fulfill!

Tuesday

Orphic Hymn

Magnanimous, unconquered, boisterous Mars,
In darts rejoicing, and in bloody wars
Fierce and untamed, whose mighty power can make
The strongest walls from their foundations shake:
Mortal destroying king, defiled with gore,
Pleased with war's dreadful and tumultuous roar:
You, human blood, and swords, and spears delight,
And the dire ruin of mad savage fight.
Stay, furious contests, and avenging strife,
Whose works with woe, embitter human life;
To lovely Venus, and to Bacchus yield,
To Ceres give the weapons of the field;
Encourage peace, to gentle works inclined,
And give abundance, with benignant mind.

Conjuration

I conjure and call upon you, you strong and good angels, in the names Yah, Yah, Yah; Heh, Heh, Heh; Vav, Hy, Hy, Ha, Ha, Ha; Vav, Vav, Vav; An, An, An; Aia, Aia, Aia; El, Ay, Elibra, Elohim, Elohim; and by the names of the high God, who has made the sea and dry land, and by his word has made the earth, and produced trees, and has set his seal upon the planets, with his precious, honored, revered and holy name; and by the name of the angels governing in the fifth house, who are subservient to the great angel Acimoy, who is strong, powerful, and honored, and by the name of his star which is called Mars, I call upon thee, Khamael, by the names above mentioned, thou great angel! who presides over the day of Mars, and by the name Adonai, the living and true God, that you assist me in accomplishing my labors!

Wednesday

Orphic Hymn

*Hermes, draw near, and to my prayer incline,
Messenger of Jove, and Maia's son divine;
Studious of contests, ruler of mankind,
With heart almighty, and a prudent mind.
Celestial messenger, of various skill,
Whose powerful arts could watchful Argus kill:
With winged feet, through air you course,
O friend of man, and prophet of discourse:
Great life-supporter, to rejoice is thine,
In arts gymnastic, and in fraud divine:
With power endued all language to explain,
Of care the looseners, and the source of gain.
Whose hand contains of blameless peace the rod,
Corucian, blessed, profitable God;
Of various speech, whose aid in works we find,
And in necessities to mortals kind:*

Conjuration

I conjure and call upon you, you strong and holy angels, good and powerful, in a strong name of fear and praise, Yah, Adonai, Elohim, Shaddai, Shaddai, Shaddai; Eheieh, Eheieh, Eheieh; Asamie, Asamie; and in the name of Adonai, the God of Israel, who has made the two great lights, and distinguished day from night for the benefit of his creatures; and by the names of all the discerning angels, governing openly in the second house before the great angel,

Tetra, strong and powerful; and by the name of his star which is Mercury; and by the name of his seal, which is that of a powerful and honored God; I call upon you, Michael, and by the names above mentioned, Oh great angel who presides over the fourth day: and by the holy name which is written in the front of Aaron, created the most high priest, and by the names of all the angels who are constant in the grace of Christ, and by the name and place of Ammaluim, that you assist me in my labors!

Thursday

Orphic Hymn

O Jove much-honored, Jove supremely great,
To you our holy rites we consecrate,
Our prayers and expiations, king divine,
For all things round thy head exalted shine.
The earth is thine, and mountains swelling high,
The sea profound, and all within the sky.
Saturnian king, descending from above,
Magnanimous, commanding, sceptered Jove;
All-parent, principle and end of all,
Whose power almighty, shakes this earthly ball;
Even Nature trembles at thy mighty nod,
Loud-sounding, armed with lightning, thundering God.
Source of abundance, purifying king,
O various-formed from whom all natures spring;
Propitious hear my prayer, give blameless health,
With peace divine, and necessary wealth.

Conjuration

I conjure and confirm upon you, you strong and holy angels, by the names Kadosh, Kadosh, Kadosh, Eschercie, Escherei, Eschercie, Hatim, Ya, strong founder of the worlds; Cantine, Jaym, Janic, Anic, Calbot, Sabbac, Berisay, Alnaym; and by the name Adonai, who created fishes and creeping things in the waters, and birds upon the face of the earth, flying towards heaven, in the fifth day; and by the names of the angels serving in the sixth host before Pastor, a holy angel, and a great and powerful prince and by the name of his star, which is Jupiter, and by the name of his seal, and by the name of Adonai, the great God, Creator of all things, and by the name of all the stars, and by their power and virtue, and by all the names aforesaid, I conjure thee, Sachiel, a great Angel, who is chief ruler of Thursday, that for me you will labor!

Friday

Orphic Hymn

*Heavenly, illustrious, laughter-loving queen,
Sea-born, night-loving, of an awful mien;
Crafty, from whom necessity first came,
Producing, nightly, all-connecting dame:
Yours is the world with harmony to join,
For all things spring from you, O power divine.
The triple Fates are ruled by thy decree,
And all productions yield alike to you:
Whatever the heavens, encircling all contain,
Earth fruit-producing, and the stormy main,
Your sway confesses, and obeys thy nod,
Awful attendant of the wintry God:
Goddess of marriage, charming to the sight,
Mother of Loves, whom banquets delight;
Source of persuasion, secret, favoring queen,
Illustrious born, apparent and unseen:
Spousal, lupercal, and to men inclined,*

<u>Luminarium</u>

Prolific, most desired, life-giving, kind:
Great scepter bearer of the Gods, 'tis thine,
Mortals in necessary bands to join;
And every tribe of savage monsters dire
In magic chains to bind, through mad desire.
Come, Cyprus-born, and to my prayer incline,
Whether exalted in the heavens you shine,
Or pleased in Syria's temple to preside,
Or over the Egyptian plains your car to guide,
Fashioned of gold; and near its sacred flood,
Fertile and famed to fix thy blessed abode;
Or if rejoicing in the azure shores,
Near where the sea with foaming billows roars,
The circling choirs of mortals, thy delight,
Or beauteous nymphs, with eyes cerulean bright,
Pleased by the dusty banks renowned of old,
To drive your rapid, two yoked car of gold;
Or if in Cyprus with thy mother fair,
Where married females praise you every year,
And beauteous virgins in the chorus join,
Adonis pure to sing and you divine;
Come, all-attractive to my prayer inclined,
For thee, I call, with holy, reverent mind.

Conjuration

I conjure and confirm upon you, you strong and holy angels, by the names On, Hey, Heyah, Yah, Yah, Shaddai, Adonai, and in the name Shaddai, who created four-footed beasts, and creeping things, and man, in the sixth day, and gave to Adam power over all creatures; wherefore blessed be the name of the Creator in his place; and by the name of the angels serving in the third host, before Dagiel, a great angel, and a strong and powerful prince, and by the name of his star, which is Venus, and by his seal which is holy; and by all the names aforesaid, I conjure you, Haniel, who is the chief ruler this day, that you will labor for me!

Saturday

Orphic Hymn

Etherial father, mighty Titan, hear,
Great fire of Gods and men, whom all revere:
Endued with various council, pure and strong,
To whom perfection and decrease belong.
Consumed by you all forms that hourly die,
By you restored, their former place supply;
The world immense in everlasting chains,
Strong and ineffable your power contains
Father of vast eternity, divine,
O mighty Saturn, various speech is thine:
Blossom of earth and of the starry skies,
Husband of Rhea, and Prometheus wife.
Obstetric Nature, venerable root,
From which the various forms of being shoot;
No parts peculiar can your power enclose,
Diffused through all, from which the world arose,
O, best of beings, of a subtle mind,
Propitious hear to holy prayers inclined;
The sacred rites benevolent attend,
And grant a blameless life, a blessed end.

Conjuration

I conjure and confirm upon you, Cassiel, Machator, and Seraquiel, strong and powerful angels; and by the name Adonai, Adonai, Adonai; Eheieh, Eheieh, Eheieh; Yehoiakim, Yehoiakim, Yehoiakim; Kadosh, Kadosh; Ima, Ima, Ima; Salay, Yah, Sar, Lord and Maker of the World, who rested on the seventh day; and by him who of his good pleasure gave the same to be observed by the children of Israel throughout their generations, that they should keep and sanctify the same, to have thereby a good reward in the world to conic; and by the names of the angels serving in the seventh host, before Booel, a great angel, and powerful prince; and by the name of his star, which is Saturn; and by his holy seal, and by the names before spoken, I conjure upon you, Cassiel, who is chief ruler of the seventh day, which is the Sabbath, that for me you will labor!

Luminarium

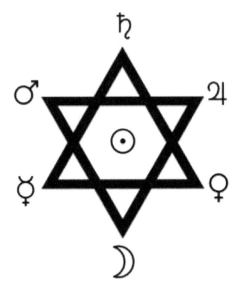

Rituals

The overall purpose of this text is to provide a series of rituals for accessing celestial powers to attain effective results in your life and for gaining knowledge from the heavenly spheres. It may seem like we've taken a little while to get to that purpose, but everything presented thus far has been a stripped-down summation of how to begin this work. The daily prayers given in the last section provide a form of preparation which will directly affect this aim in your life.

With the minimal description given above you will be ready to jump in directly. There is no need for the armchair, no need for the sidelines. Assuming you've gathered the tools and done a little preparation, today you're ready to conjure an angel and ask it for help with whatever needs you have, or for guidance in the various areas of life.

When you conjure the angels and the aerial spirits, ask them to agree to come quickly when called by simple prayers. This will allow you to use their aid in the work which will follow these rituals. Ask them by what means to call them, if there are special names or seals or prayers that you may use to more simply call upon them. For some purposes you will want to run a full ritual like those provided here. At other times a simple prayer, or the use of simple means provided by the angel, will be sufficient, along with the psalms, to use the talismans and other spell work.

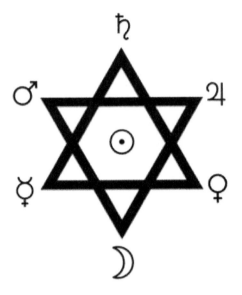

Timing

When selecting the time for your ritual there are a few options to consider. Each hour of the day is ruled by a spirit, or it may be considered that the hour has a spirit and is itself a living power. Each day, those spirits take on a planetary nature based upon the sequence of the hours and the planetary rays associated with the rising of the Sun. From this process we have the planetary hours, or the hours in which these spirits empower a particular planet's force and facilitate spirits operating with ease and more power. The most basic approach to timing your ritual is to begin in the appropriate planetary hour on the appropriate planetary day. Thus, if you wanted help finding a stable job you might call upon Sachiel, the archangel of Jupiter, during the hour of Jupiter on a Thursday. If you have need to work with a particular spirit on a day not ruled by that spirit, then working during that spirit's planetary hour is still an option. For example, if something occurs on Sunday for which you need to call upon Sachiel and do not have time to wait until Thursday, then one of the hours of Jupiter which occurs on Sunday would be acceptable as well.

The hours are calculated by determining the time of sunrise, sunset, and the next day's sunrise. Divide the time between sunrise and sunset into twelve equal parts and you have the length of the daytime planetary hours. Do the same for the time between sunset and the next day's sunrise and you have the length of the night time planetary hours. The first hour begins at sunrise and accords to the planet which rules the day. Thus, sunrise on Sunday is the hour of the Sun. The next hour follows the order of the planets, so next is the hour of Venus, then Mercury, and so forth.

An alternate means of selecting the time would be to consider when the planet reaches the highest point in the sky. The hour leading into that moment would also be a fortuitous hour for the planet, particularly on the day ruled by the planet.

If you are skilled in electional astrology you could, alternatively, conjure based upon some moment which is well aspected for the planet, or in which the planet is dignified. For example, if the planet is in a degree of the zodiac matching to a decan ruled by the planet.

Sometimes our schedules do not allow for selecting a time based upon the planetary hour or an electional moment, but we still want to use the physical position of the planet as part of the way in which we invoke time. In such an instance, determine the place in the zodiac in which the planet is currently residing. Then invoke the zodiacal space so that the zodiacal sphere is defining the time of the ritual and therefore the planet and the ritual are inhabiting the same space.

The process for this is simple. Each zodiac sign has an element and a ruling planet. Before beginning your conjuration, after you have called upon your ancestors, go to each quarter and trace the sign of the ruling element and planet for the sign in which the planet pertaining to your ritual resides at the time your ritual is beginning. Trace the signs and call upon the presence of the angel who rules that zodiacal sign. Therefore, if you are doing a ritual of Mars and Mars is in Libra at the time of your ritual you would go to each quarter, and trace a symbol of Air, a symbol of Venus, and call upon Zuriel. In each quarter, seal the invocation with the sign of the cross and the seal of the zodiacal sign. Your ritual is now occurring within the light of the sign in which your planet resides, and thus, you and the planet are within the same space.

Cosmological Note

Magic is often the application of particular elements of one's understanding of the nature of existence. At times this includes understanding how existence begins and how it ends. The structure of the ritual we are providing is no different.

At the beginning of the ritual the magician will cleanse the space with the khernips, in which he has mixed fire and water. This mixing signifies the primal state of creation, the chaotic mist from which everything stems. He will light the four candles on his altar, which are the four potentials that become the elements: hot, cold, moist, and dry. He will burn incense, and with fire from earth he will release air and that air will give shape to the mist. His words, like the air of the incense, will further shape the mist. He will call Night, from whom creation came, and Eros, who stirred the creative faculty and binds the heavenly nature of magical acts to the physical nature of the world. He will call Hekate, who will give access to the spirit world and to magic. The ancestors will provide leverage in the spirit world and assistance to the magician, as will the Guardian Angel.

The magician will invoke the lamp as a means of invoking the Guardian Angel, such that its light will illuminate the magician and allow greater ability to perceive the spirits and understand communication with them. The interaction with the spirit is transmitted through the light of one's own Guardian Angel, thus the Angel transmits and translates the communication so that it is clear for the magician.

The Pre-Ritual

As stated above, prior to the beginning of the ritual the magician will perform a khernips to cleanse themselves, and then put on their ritual attire. There are steps to take in putting on the attire and additional steps to do before the ritual begins. We will outline those here rather than include them with the individual ritual scripts.

Prior to beginning, the magician will perform the khernips outside of his ritual space. Begin with a bowl of water and herbs. Drop smoldering herbs, or wood or rope into the water and say: kherniptosai

Then strip down and wash your hands, face, underarms, genitals and feet.

Now you may put on your ritual attire. As you do so pray:

I will go to the altar of the Lord, who was the joy of my youth.

Psalm 102 *(1) Hear my prayer, O Lord, and let my cry come unto thee. (2) Hide not thy face from me in the day when I am in trouble; incline thine ear unto me: in the day when I call answer me speedily. (3) For my days are consumed like smoke, and my bones are burned as an hearth. (4) My heart is smitten, and withered like grass; so that I forget to eat my bread. (5) By reason of the voice of my groaning my bones cleave to my skin. (6) I am like a pelican of the wilderness: I am like an owl of the desert. (7) I watch, and am as a sparrow alone upon the house top. (8) Mine enemies reproach me all the day; and they that are mad against me are sworn against me. (9) For I have eaten ashes like bread, and mingled my drink with weeping, (10) Because of thine indignation and thy wrath: for thou hast lifted me up, and cast me down. (11) My days are like a shadow that declineth; and I am withered like grass. (12) But thou, O Lord, shalt endure for ever; and thy remembrance unto all generations. (13) Thou shalt arise, and have mercy upon Zion: for the time to favour her, yea, the set time, is come. (14) For thy servants take pleasure in her stones, and favour the dust thereof. (15) So the heathen shall fear the name of the Lord, and all the kings of the earth thy glory. (16) When the Lord shall build up Zion, he shall appear in his glory. (17) He will regard the prayer of the destitute, and not despise their prayer. (18) This shall be written for the generation to come: and the people which shall be created shall praise the Lord. (19) For he hath looked down from the height of his sanctuary; from heaven did the Lord behold the earth; (20) To hear the groaning of the prisoner; to loose those that are appointed to death; (21) To declare the name of the Lord in Zion, and his praise in Jerusalem; (22) When the people are gathered together, and the kingdoms, to serve the Lord. (23) He weakened my strength in the way; he shortened my days. (24) I said, O my God, take me not away in the midst of my days: thy years are throughout all generations. (25) Of old hast thou laid the foundation of the earth: and the heavens are the work of thy hands. (26) They shall perish, but thou shalt endure: yea, all of them shall wax old like a garment; as a vesture shalt thou change them, and they shall be changed: (27) But thou art the same, and thy years shall have no end. (28) The children of thy servants shall continue, and their seed shall be established before thee.*

Ancor, Amacor, Amides, Theodonias, Anitor, by the merits of your Angel, Oh Lord, I will put on the Garments of Salvation, that this which I desire I may bring to effect: through You the most holy Adonai, whose kingdom endures for ever and ever. Amen.

Once you have donned your ritual attire, go to your ritual space. Light your lamp, dimly. Make a prayer from your heart for the presence and assistance of your Guardian Angel. Once you feel the angel's presence, make an extemporaneous confession. This confession can have an element of unburdening yourself of concerns and stresses; it should also acknowledge things you do which are problematic or which undermine your success, your commitment to your magical work, or which may make difficult the goal for which you are conjuring. When you finish the confession, make a prayer from the heart for your angel to guide you, and state your commitment to rise above these issues and solve them.

Once this is done, take a few moments to calm and center yourself, then begin the ritual.

The Rituals

Spirits and Powers of the Sphere of Sol

The archangel of Sol is Raphael. Varcan is the king of the aerial spirits of Sol with Tuas, Andas, and Cynabal as his ministers. The aerial spirits come on the North wind.

The seal for Raphael is:

The seal for Varcan is:

The Pentacle for Solar Spirits is:

The Solar Spirits can aid in obtaining riches, causing favor or dignities, establishing imperium, raising men to honors, establishing friendships, dissolving animosity, they can take away illness and provide healing.

Opening

The magician has completed the pre-ritual preparations and is at the altar with his lamp lit, dimly.

The magician lights the bundle for the khernips drops it in the water and says:

Kherniptosai

The magician takes the khernips and encircles around the working space. After replacing the bowl the magician lights the four candles and then lights the incense. The magician then circles the working space with the incense and blows the incense over the altar and the tools before replacing it.

The magician touches the ground and says:

Powers of this time and place, spirits of nature be with me, make open the ways of magic and accept my thanks for your aid.

Invocation of The Divine Natural Powers

The magician raises their hands to heaven and invokes Nyx

Nyx, parent goddess, source of sweet repose,
from whom at first both Gods and men arose,
Hear, blessed Venus, deck'd with starry light,
in sleep's deep silence dwelling Ebon night!
Dreams and soft case attend thy dusky train,
pleas'd with the length'ned gloom and feastful strain.
Dissolving anxious care, the friend of Mirth,
with darkling coursers riding round the earth.
Goddess of phantoms and of shadowy play,
whose drowsy pow'r divides the nat'ral day:
By Fate's decree you constant send the light

to deepest hell, remote from mortal sight
For dire Necessity which nought withstands,
invests the world with adamantine bands.
Be present, Goddess, to thy suppliant's pray'r,
desir'd by all, whom all alike revere,
Blessed, benevolent, with friendly aid
dispell the fears of Twilight's dreadful shade.

The magician now pours wine in the offering cup for Nyx and then raises hands again to invoke Eros

I Call great Eros, source of sweet delight,
holy and pure, and lovely to the sight;
Darting, and wing'd, impetuous fierce desire,
with Gods and mortals playing, wand'ring fire:
Cautious, and two-fold, keeper of the keys
of heav'n and earth, the air, and spreading seas;
Of all that Ceres' fertile realms contains,
by which th' all-parent Goddess life sustains,
Or dismal Tartarus is doom'd to keep,
widely extended, or the sounding, deep;
For thee, all Nature's various realms obey,
who rul'st alone, with universal sway.
Come, blessed pow'r, regard these mystic fires,
and far avert, unlawful mad desires.

The magician now pours wine in the offering cup for Eros and then raises hands again to invoke Hekate

Hekate Einodia, Trioditis, lovely dame,
of earthly, watery, and celestial frame,
sepulchral, in a saffron veil arrayed,
pleased with dark ghosts that wander through the shade;
Daughter of Perses, solitary goddess, hail!
The world's key-bearer, never doomed to fail;
in stags rejoicing, huntress, nightly seen,
and drawn by bulls, unconquerable queen;

Leader, Nymphe, nurse, on mountains wandering,
hear the suppliants who with holy rites thy power revere,
and to the herdsman with a favouring mind draw near.

The magician pours wine in the offering cup for Hekate

Invocation of the Ancestors

The magician now calls upon the ancestors.

The magician knocks three times on the ancestor altar and then touches the coins

Charon, ferryman, I call upon you bring forth my ancestors and allies that you and they may partake of these offerings and they may aid me in this magic. I call upon Hades and Persephone to bring forth my ancestors and strengthen them and partake with them of these offerings.

The magician lights frankincense and myrrh and says:

I give this that the world may be made sweet for you, that through frankincense you remember that you are holy and through myrrh you find strength in death

The magician lights the two candles for the unnamed dead saying

For those ancestors by blood not named, and those ancestors not by blood not named

The magician lights the remaining candles naming each respective ancestor

The magician now briefly thanks the ancestors and explains the intention for the day

The Elementals (Optional)

Should the magician choose to call upon the aid of the elementals the appropriate elemental prayer may be inserted here.

Invocation of the Lamp

The magician places the coin, the magnet, and the wood in the scrying bowl, and traces a circle around the space with the incense, the magician then places the red cloth upon their head

The magician makes this prayer to call upon their angel while focused upon the lamp, the magician turns up the lamp's light.

Hail serpent and stout lion, natural sources of fire
Hail clear water and lofty-leafed tree
And you who gather up clover from golden fields of beans
And who cause gentle foam to gush forth from pure mouths.
Scarab who drive the orb of fertile fire,
O self-engendered one
Because you are Two-syllabled, AE,
and are the first appearing one
Nod me assent I pray, because your mystic symbols I declare,
EO AI OY AMERR OOUOTH IYIOE MARMARAUOTH LAILAM SOUMARTA
Be gracious unto me first-father and May you yourself send strength as my companion.
Stay allied, lord, and listen to me, through the charm that produces the vision, which I [NAME] do today IY EYE OO AEE IAEE AIAE E AI EY EIE OOOOO EY EO IAOAI

I call upon you, the living god, fiery, invisible, begetter or light IAEL PEIPTA PHOS ZA PAI PHTHENTHA PHOSZA PYRI BELIA IAO IAO EYO OEE A OY EOI A E E I O Y O give me strength, rouse your daimon, enter into this fire, fill it with a divine spirit and show me your might. Let there be

opened for me the house of the all-powerful god ALBALAL who is in this light. Let there be light, breadth, depth, length, height, brightness, and let him who is inside shine through, the lord BOUEL PHTHA PHTHA PHTHAEL PHTHA ABAI BAINCHOOOCH, now now immediately, immediately, quickly, quickly.

I conjure you holy light, holy brightness, by the wholy names which I have spoken and am now going to speak. By IAO SABAOTH ARBATHIAO SESENGENBARPHARAGGES ABLANATHANALBA ALRAMMACHAMARI AI AI IAO AX AX INAX remain by me in this present hour, until, I pray to the god, and learn about the things I desire.

The magician whispers these names into the scrying bowl:

Atzam, Tzoalakoum, Geamai, Satzyne, Kalesaines, Ton, Tapesmas, Taphydou, Elylpe, Syltan, Gialoti, Mpalontzem, Thara, Pakhakhesesan, Sylbakhama, Mousamoukhana, Araga, Rhasai, Rhagana, Obras, Ouboragoras, Tzoupa, Biapophkha, Tambalakhakem, Parakhematzoum, Tou, Itana, Baphoutia, Pakhakhe, Tanretokous, Nastratie, Parakhematzoum, Tou, Itana, Baphoutia, Pakhakhe, Tanretokous, Nastratie, Pakhakhyelea, Tybalotze, Enkaika, Parpara, Oumebras, Khematzoum

Conjuration of the Angel

The magician holds the wand and the vessel of oil and conjures the angel

Hear golden Titan, whose eternal eye
With broad survey, illumines all the sky.
Self-born, unwearied in diffusing light,
And to all eyes the mirror of delight:
Lord of the seasons, with your fiery car
And leaping coursers, beaming light from far:

Luminarium

With thy right hand the source of morning light,
And with thy left the father of the night.
Agile and vigorous, venerable Sun,
Fiery and bright around the heavens you run.
Foe to the wicked, but the good man's guide,
Over all his steps propitious you preside:
With various founding, golden lyre, 'tis mine
To fill the world with harmony divine.
Father of ages, guide of prosperous deeds,
The world's commander, borne by lucid steeds,
Immortal Jove, all-searching, bearing light,
Source of existence, pure and fiery bright
Bearer of fruit, almighty lord of years,
Agile and warm, whom every power reveres.
Great eye of Nature and the starry skies,
Doomed with immortal flames to set and rise
Dispensing justice, lover of the stream,
The world's great despot, and over all supreme.
Faithful defender, and the eye of right,
Of steeds the ruler, and of life the light:
With founding whip four fiery steeds you guide,
When in the car of day you glorious ride.
Propitious on these mystic labors shine,
And bless thy suppliants with a life divine.

I conjure and confirm upon you, you strong and holy angels of God, in the name Adonai, Eheieh, Eheieh, Eya, which is he who was, and is, and is to come, Eye, Abray; and in the name Shaddai, Kadosh, Kadosh, sitting on high upon the Kerubim; and by the great name of God himself, strong and powerful, who is exalted above all the heavens; Eye, Saraye, who created the world, the heavens, the earth, the sea, and all that is in them, in the first day, and scaled them with his holy name Phaa; and by the name of the angels who rule in the fourth heaven, and serve before the most mighty Salamia, an angel great and honorable; and by the name of his star, which is Sol, and by his sign, and by the immense name of the living God, and by all the names aforesaid, I conjure you, Raphael, O great angel! who is chief ruler of this day; and by the name Adonai, the God of Israel, I conjure you, O Raphael! that you will labor for me, and fulfill all my petitions according to my will and desire in my cause and business!

The magician pours the oil into the water within the scrying bowl and commands the angel to appear in the vessel.

At this point the magician may ask the angel for needed information or make a request of the angel.

Conjuration of the Aerial Spirits (Optional)

Should the magician desire to call upon the aerial spirits the magician requests the assistance of the angel in doing so then while holding the wand and the pentacle makes this conjuration.

I conjure you Oh Mighty and potent Prince Varcan who rules as king in the dominion of the North. I conjure you Varcan in the name of Raphael that you appear swiftly and in pleasing form with all your attending ministers in this vessel and fulfill all the things I ask of you.

This conjuration is recited until the spirit and his ministers arrive. When they arrive the magician must show them the seal of the King and the Pentacle of Solomon and say:

Behold the Pentacle of Solomon which I have brought before your presence! Behold the exorcist in this rite of the exorcism, who is who is fortified by the providence of the Most High God, fearlessly he has called you by the powerful force of this exorcism. Therefore come quickly by the virtue of these names, Aye, Saraye, Aye, Saraye, Aye, Saraye, do not delay to come, by the name of the True Eternal and Living

God, Eloy, Archima, Rabur, and through this Pentacle which has been presented and powerfully rules over you and through the virtue of the Heavenly Spirits, of your Lords, and by the person of the Exorcist who has conjured you, come quickly and obediently to your master who is called Octinomos.

After calling the aerial spirits and making your petitions end the ceremony by issuing the license to depart.

License to Depart

+In the name of the Father + the Son + and the Holy Spirit go now in peace to your dwelling and let there be peace between us so that you may be ready to come again when called.

Spirits and Powers of the Sphere of Luna

The archangel of Luna is Gabriel. Arcan is the king of the aerial spirits of Luna with Bilet, Missabu, and Abuzaha as his ministers. The aerial spirits come on the West wind.

The seal for Gabriel is:

The seal for Arcan is:

The Pentacle for Lunar Spirits is:

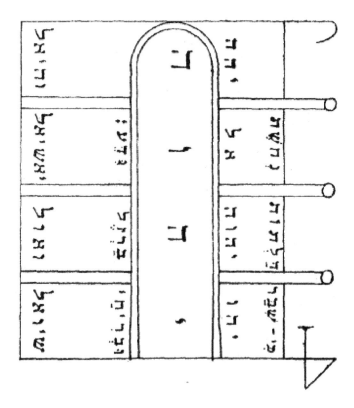

The Spirits of the Moon provide silver, they aid in travel, they can manipulate emotions, create illusions, influence dreams, disclose and convey secrets, and provide information on the future

Opening

The magician has completed the pre-ritual preparations and is at the altar with his lamp lit, dimly.

The magician lights the bundle for the khernips drops it in the water and says:

Kherniptosai

The magician takes the khernips and encircles around the working space. After replacing the bowl the magician lights the four candles and then lights the incense. The magician then circles the working space with the incense and blows the incense over the altar and the tools before replacing it.

The magician touches the ground and says:

Powers of this time and place, spirits of nature be with me, make open the ways of magic and accept my thanks for your aid.

Invocation of The Divine Natural Powers

The magician raises their hands to heaven and invokes Nyx

Nyx, parent goddess, source of sweet repose,
from whom at first both Gods and men arose,
Hear, blessed Venus, deck'd with starry light,
in sleep's deep silence dwelling Ebon night!
Dreams and soft case attend thy dusky train,
pleas'd with the length'ned gloom and feastful strain.
Dissolving anxious care, the friend of Mirth,
with darkling coursers riding round the earth.
Goddess of phantoms and of shadowy play,
whose drowsy pow'r divides the nat'ral day:
By Fate's decree you constant send the light

to deepest hell, remote from mortal sight
For dire Necessity which nought withstands,
invests the world with adamantine bands.
Be present, Goddess, to thy suppliant's pray'r,
desir'd by all, whom all alike revere,
Blessed, benevolent, with friendly aid
dispell the fears of Twilight's dreadful shade.

The magician now pours wine in the offering cup for Nyx and then raises hands again to invoke Eros

I Call great Eros, source of sweet delight,
holy and pure, and lovely to the sight;
Darting, and wing'd, impetuous fierce desire,
with Gods and mortals playing, wand'ring fire:
Cautious, and two-fold, keeper of the keys
of heav'n and earth, the air, and spreading seas;
Of all that Ceres' fertile realms contains,
by which th' all-parent Goddess life sustains,
Or dismal Tartarus is doom'd to keep,
widely extended, or the sounding, deep;
For thee, all Nature's various realms obey,
who rul'st alone, with universal sway.
Come, blessed pow'r, regard these mystic fires,
and far avert, unlawful mad desires.

The magician now pours wine in the offering cup for Eros and then raises hands again to invoke Hekate

Hekate Einodia, Trioditis, lovely dame,
of earthly, watery, and celestial frame,
sepulchral, in a saffron veil arrayed,
pleased with dark ghosts that wander through the shade;
Daughter of Perses, solitary goddess, hail!
The world's key-bearer, never doomed to fail;
in stags rejoicing, huntress, nightly seen,
and drawn by bulls, unconquerable queen;

*Leader, Nymphe, nurse, on mountains wandering,
hear the suppliants who with holy rites thy power revere,
and to the herdsman with a favouring mind draw near.*

The magician pours wine in the offering cup for Hekate

Invocation of the Ancestors

The magician now calls upon the ancestors.

The magician knocks three times on the ancestor altar and then touches the coins

Charon, ferryman, I call upon you bring forth my ancestors and allies that you and they may partake of these offerings and they may aid me in this magic. I call upon Hades and Persephone to bring forth my ancestors and strengthen them and partake with them of these offerings.

The magician lights frankincense and myrrh and says:

I give this that the world may be made sweet for you, that through frankincense you remember that you are holy and through myrrh you find strength in death

The magician lights the two candles for the unnamed dead saying

For those ancestors by blood not named, and those ancestors not by blood not named

The magician lights the remaining candles naming each respective ancestor

The magician now briefly thanks the ancestors and explains the intention for the day

Luminarium

The Elementals (Optional)

Should the magician choose to call upon the aid of the elementals the appropriate elemental prayer may be inserted here.

Invocation of the Lamp

The magician places the coin, the magnet, and the wood in the scrying bowl, and traces a circle around the space with the incense, the magician then places the red cloth upon their head

The magician makes this prayer to call upon their angel while focused upon the lamp, the magician turns up the lamp's light.

Hail serpent and stout lion, natural sources of fire
Hail clear water and lofty-leafed tree
And you who gather up clover from golden fields of beans
And who cause gentle foam to gush forth from pure mouths.
Scarab who drive the orb of fertile fire,
O self-engendered one
Because you are Two-syllabled, AE,
and are the first appearing one
Nod me assent I pray, because your mystic symbols I declare,
EO AI OY AMERR OOUOTH IYIOE MARMARAUOTH LAILAM SOUMARTA
Be gracious unto me first-father and May you yourself send strength as my companion.
Stay allied, lord, and listen to me, through the charm that produces the vision, which I [NAME] do today IY EYE OO AEE IAEE AIAE E AI EY EIE OOOOO EY EO IAOAI

I call upon you, the living god, fiery, invisible, begetter or light IAEL PEIPTA PHOS ZA PAI PHTHENTHA PHOSZA PYRI BELIA IAO IAO EYO OEE A OY EOI A E E I O Y O give me strength, rouse your daimon, enter into this fire, fill it with a divine spirit and show me your might. Let there be

opened for me the house of the all-powerful god ALBALAL who is in this light. Let there be light, breadth, depth, length, height, brightness, and let him who is inside shine through, the lord BOUEL PHTHA PHTHA PHTHAEL PHTHA ABAI BAINCHOOOCH, now now immediately, immediately, quickly, quickly.

I conjure you holy light, holy brightness, by the wholy names which I have spoken and am now going to speak. By IAO SABAOTH ARBATHIAO SESENGENBARPHARAGGES ABLANATHANALBA ALRAMMACHAMARI AI AI IAO AX AX INAX remain by me in this present hour, until, I pray to the god, and learn about the things I desire.

The magician whispers these names into the scrying bowl:

Atzam, Tzoalakoum, Geamai, Satzyne, Kalesaines, Ton, Tapesmas, Taphydou, Elylpe, Syltan, Gialoti, Mpalontzem, Thara, Pakhakhesesan, Sylbakhama, Mousamoukhana, Araga, Rhasai, Rhagana, Obras, Ouboragoras, Tzoupa, Biapophkha, Tambalakhakem, Parakhematzoum, Tou, Itana, Baphoutia, Pakhakhe, Tanretokous, Nastratie, Parakhematzoum, Tou, Itana, Baphoutia, Pakhakhe, Tanretokous, Nastratie, Pakhakhyelea, Tybalotze, Enkaika, Parpara, Oumebras, Khematzoum

Conjuration of the Angel

The magician holds the wand and the vessel of oil and conjures the angel

HEAR, Goddess queen, diffusing silver light,
Bull-horned and wandering through the gloom of Night.
With stars surrounded, and with circuit wide
Night's torch extending, through the heavens you ride:
Female and Male with borrowed rays you shine,
And now full orbed, now tending to decline.

Luminarium

Mother of ages, fruit-producing Moon,
Whose amber orb makes Night's reflected noon:
Lover of horses, splendid, queen of Night,
All-seeing power bedecked with starry light.
Lover of vigilance, the foe of strife,
In peace rejoicing, and a prudent life:
Fair lamp of Night, its ornament and friend,
Who gives to Nature's works their destined end.
Queen of the stars, all-wife Artemis hail!
Decked with a graceful robe and shining veil;
Come, blessed Goddess, prudent, starry, bright,
Come moonlit lamp with chaste and splendid light,
Shine on these sacred rites with prosperous rays,
And pleased accept thy suppliant's mystic praise.

I conjure and confirm upon you, strong and good angels, in the name Adonai, Adonai, Adonai, Adonai, Eheieh, Eheieh, Eheieh; Kadosh, Kadosh, Kadosh, Yehoiakim, Yehoiakim, Yah, Yah, strong Yah, who appeared in mount Sinai with the glorification of king Adonai, Shaddai, Tzavot, Anathay, Yah, Yah, Yah, Maranata, Abimelek, Jeia, who created the sea, and all lakes and waters, in the second day, which are above the heavens and in the earth, and scaled the sea in his high name, and gave it its bounds beyond which it cannot pass; and by the names of the angels who rule in the first legion, and who serve Orphaniel, a great, precious, and honorable angel, and by the name of his star which is Luna, and by all the names aforesaid, I conjure thee, Gabriel, who art chief ruler of Monday, the second day, that for me you shall labor and fulfill!

The magician pours the oil into the water within the scrying bowl and commands the angel to appear in the vessel.

At this point the magician may ask the angel for needed information or make a request of the angel.

Conjuration of the Aerial Spirits (Optional)

Should the magician desire to call upon the aerial spirits the magician requests the assistance of the angel in doing so then while holding the wand and the pentacle makes this conjuration.

I conjure you Oh Mighty and potent Prince Arcan who rules as king in the dominion of the West. I conjure you Arcan in the name of Gabriel that you appear swiftly and in pleasing form with all your attending ministers in this vessel and fulfill all the things I ask of you.

This conjuration is recited until the spirit and his ministers arrive. When they arrive the magician must show them the seal of the King and the Pentacle of Solomon and say:

Behold the Pentacle of Solomon which I have brought before your presence! Behold the exorcist in this rite of the exorcism, who is who is fortified by the providence of the Most High God, fearlessly he has called you by the powerful force of this exorcism. Therefore come quickly by the virtue of these names, Aye, Saraye, Aye, Saraye, Aye, Saraye, do not delay to come, by the name of the True Eternal and Living God, Eloy, Archima, Rabur, and through this Pentacle which has been presented and powerfully rules over you and through the virtue of the Heavenly Spirits, of your Lords, and by the person of the Exorcist who has conjured you, come quickly and obediently to your master who is called Octinomos.

After calling the aerial spirits and making your petitions end the ceremony by issuing the license to depart.

License to Depart

+In the name of the Father + the Son + and the Holy Spirit go now in peace to your dwelling and let there be peace between us so that you may be ready to come again when called.

Spirits and Powers of the Sphere of Mars

The archangel of Mars is Khamael. Samax is the king of the aerial spirits of Mars with Carmax, Ismoli, and Paffran as his ministers. The aerial spirits come on the East wind.

The seal for Khamael is:

The seal for Samax is:

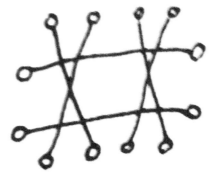

The Pentacle for Martial Spirits is:

The Martial spirits should be called to incite war, to cause death, to cause combustion, to bring soldiers, to create illness or health, for success in sports, for victory, for strength and fitness, and for issues related to vehicles, weapons and machines.

Opening

The magician has completed the pre-ritual preparations and is at the altar with his lamp lit, dimly.

The magician lights the bundle for the khernips drops it in the water and says:

Kherniptosai

The magician takes the khernips and encircles around the working space. After replacing the bowl the magician lights the four candles and then lights the incense. The magician then circles the working space with the incense and blows the incense over the altar and the tools before replacing it.

The magician touches the ground and says:

Powers of this time and place, spirits of nature be with me, make open the ways of magic and accept my thanks for your aid.

Invocation of The Divine Natural Powers

The magician raises their hands to heaven and invokes Nyx

Nyx, parent goddess, source of sweet repose,
from whom at first both Gods and men arose,
Hear, blessed Venus, deck'd with starry light,
in sleep's deep silence dwelling Ebon night!
Dreams and soft case attend thy dusky train,
pleas'd with the length'ned gloom and feastful strain.
Dissolving anxious care, the friend of Mirth,
with darkling coursers riding round the earth.
Goddess of phantoms and of shadowy play,
whose drowsy pow'r divides the nat'ral day:
By Fate's decree you constant send the light

Luminarium

to deepest hell, remote from mortal sight
For dire Necessity which nought withstands,
invests the world with adamantine bands.
Be present, Goddess, to thy suppliant's pray'r,
desir'd by all, whom all alike revere,
Blessed, benevolent, with friendly aid
dispell the fears of Twilight's dreadful shade.

The magician now pours wine in the offering cup for Nyx and then raises hands again to invoke Eros

I Call great Eros, source of sweet delight,
holy and pure, and lovely to the sight;
Darting, and wing'd, impetuous fierce desire,
with Gods and mortals playing, wand'ring fire:
Cautious, and two-fold, keeper of the keys
of heav'n and earth, the air, and spreading seas;
Of all that Ceres' fertile realms contains,
by which th' all-parent Goddess life sustains,
Or dismal Tartarus is doom'd to keep,
widely extended, or the sounding, deep;
For thee, all Nature's various realms obey,
who rul'st alone, with universal sway.
Come, blessed pow'r, regard these mystic fires,
and far avert, unlawful mad desires.

The magician now pours wine in the offering cup for Eros and then raises hands again to invoke Hekate

Hekate Einodia, Trioditis, lovely dame,
of earthly, watery, and celestial frame,
sepulchral, in a saffron veil arrayed,
pleased with dark ghosts that wander through the shade;
Daughter of Perses, solitary goddess, hail!
The world's key-bearer, never doomed to fail;
in stags rejoicing, huntress, nightly seen,
and drawn by bulls, unconquerable queen;

Leader, Nymphe, nurse, on mountains wandering,
hear the suppliants who with holy rites thy power revere,
and to the herdsman with a favouring mind draw near.

The magician pours wine in the offering cup for Hekate

Invocation of the Ancestors

The magician now calls upon the ancestors.

The magician knocks three times on the ancestor altar and then touches the coins

Charon, ferryman, I call upon you bring forth my ancestors and allies that you and they may partake of these offerings and they may aid me in this magic. I call upon Hades and Persephone to bring forth my ancestors and strengthen them and partake with them of these offerings.

The magician lights frankincense and myrrh and says:

I give this that the world may be made sweet for you, that through frankincense you remember that you are holy and through myrrh you find strength in death

The magician lights the two candles for the unnamed dead saying

For those ancestors by blood not named, and those ancestors not by blood not named

The magician lights the remaining candles naming each respective ancestor

The magician now briefly thanks the ancestors and explains the intention for the day

Luminarium

The Elementals (Optional)

Should the magician choose to call upon the aid of the elementals the appropriate elemental prayer may be inserted here.

Invocation of the Lamp

The magician places the coin, the magnet, and the wood in the scrying bowl, and traces a circle around the space with the incense, the magician then places the red cloth upon their head

The magician makes this prayer to call upon their angel while focused upon the lamp, the magician turns up the lamp's light.

Hail serpent and stout lion, natural sources of fire
Hail clear water and lofty-leafed tree
And you who gather up clover from golden fields of beans
And who cause gentle foam to gush forth from pure mouths.
Scarab who drive the orb of fertile fire,
O self-engendered one
Because you are Two-syllabled, AE,
 and are the first appearing one
Nod me assent I pray, because your mystic symbols I declare,
EO AI OY AMERR OOUOTH IYIOE MARMARAUOTH LAILAM SOUMARTA
Be gracious unto me first-father and May you yourself send strength as my companion.
Stay allied, lord, and listen to me, through the charm that produces the vision, which I [NAME] do today IY EYE OO AEE IAEE AIAE E AI EY EIE OOOOO EY EO IAOAI

I call upon you, the living god, fiery, invisible, begetter or light IAEL PEIPTA PHOS ZA PAI PHTHENTHA PHOSZA PYRI BELIA IAO IAO EYO OEE A OY EOI A E E I O Y O give me strength, rouse your daimon, enter into this fire, fill it with a divine spirit and show me your might. Let there be

opened for me the house of the all-powerful god ALBALAL who is in this light. Let there be light, breadth, depth, length, height, brightness, and let him who is inside shine through, the lord BOUEL PHTHA PHTHA PHTHAEL PHTHA ABAI BAINCHOOOCH, now now immediately, immediately, quickly, quickly.

I conjure you holy light, holy brightness, by the wholy names which I have spoken and am now going to speak. By IAO SABAOTH ARBATHIAO SESENGENBARPHARAGGES ABLANATHANALBA ALRAMMACHAMARI AI AI IAO AX AX INAX remain by me in this present hour, until, I pray to the god, and learn about the things I desire.

The magician whispers these names into the scrying bowl:

Atzam, Tzoalakoum, Geamai, Satzyne, Kalesaines, Ton, Tapesmas, Taphydou, Elylpe, Syltan, Gialoti, Mpalontzem, Thara, Pakhakhesesan, Sylbakhama, Mousamoukhana, Araga, Rhasai, Rhagana, Obras, Ouboragoras, Tzoupa, Biapophkha, Tambalakhakem, Parakhematzoum, Tou, Itana, Baphoutia, Pakhakhe, Tanretokous, Nastratie, Parakhematzoum, Tou, Itana, Baphoutia, Pakhakhe, Tanretokous, Nastratie, Pakhakhyelea, Tybalotze, Enkaika, Parpara, Oumebras, Khematzoum

Conjuration of the Angel

The magician holds the wand and the vessel of oil and conjures the angel

Magnanimous, unconquered, boisterous Mars,
In darts rejoicing, and in bloody wars
Fierce and untamed, whose mighty power can make
The strongest walls from their foundations shake:
Mortal destroying king, defiled with gore,
Pleased with war's dreadful and tumultuous roar:

You, human blood, and swords, and spears delight,
And the dire ruin of mad savage fight.
Stay, furious contests, and avenging strife,
Whose works with woe, embitter human life;
To lovely Venus, and to Bacchus yield,
To Ceres give the weapons of the field;
Encourage peace, to gentle works inclined,
And give abundance, with benignant mind.

I conjure and call upon you, you strong and good angels, in the names Yah, Yah, Yah; Heh, Heh, Heh; Vav, Hy, Hy, Ha, Ha, Ha; Vav, Vav, Vav; An, An, An; Aia, Aia, Aia; El, Ay, Elibra, Elohim, Elohim; and by the names of the high God, who has made the sea and dry land, and by his word has made the earth, and produced trees, and has set his seal upon the planets, with his precious, honored, revered and holy name; and by the name of the angels governing in the fifth house, who are subservient to the great angel Acimoy, who is strong, powerful, and honored, and by the name of his star which is called Mars, I call upon thee, Khamael, by the names above mentioned, thou great angel! who presides over the day of Mars, and by the name Adonai, the living and true God, that you assist me in accomplishing my labors!

The magician pours the oil into the water within the scrying bowl and commands the angel to appear in the vessel.

At this point the magician may ask the angel for needed information or make a request of the angel.

Conjuration of the Aerial Spirits (Optional)

Should the magician desire to call upon the aerial spirits the magician requests the assistance of the angel in doing so then while holding the wand and the pentacle makes this conjuration.

I conjure you Oh Mighty and potent Prince Samax who rules as king in the dominion of the East. I conjure you Samax in the name of Khamael that you appear swiftly and in pleasing form with all your attending ministers in this vessel and fulfill all the things I ask of you.

This conjuration is recited until the spirit and his ministers arrive. When they arrive the magician must show them the seal of the King and the Pentacle of Solomon and say:

Behold the Pentacle of Solomon which I have brought before your presence! Behold the exorcist in this rite of the exorcism, who is who is fortified by the providence of the Most High God, fearlessly he has called you by the powerful force of this exorcism. Therefore come quickly by the virtue of these names, Aye, Saraye, Aye, Saraye, Aye, Saraye, do not delay to come, by the name of the True Eternal and Living God, Eloy, Archima, Rabur, and through this Pentacle which has been presented and powerfully rules over you and through the virtue of the Heavenly Spirits, of your Lords, and by the person of the Exorcist who has conjured you, come quickly and obediently to your master who is called Octinomos.

After calling the aerial spirits and making your petitions end the ceremony by issuing the license to depart.

License to Depart

+In the name of the Father + the Son + and the Holy Spirit go now in peace to your dwelling and let there be peace between us so that you may be ready to come again when called.

Spirits and Powers of the Sphere of Mercury

The archangel of Mercury is Michael. Mediat is the king of the aerial spirits of Mercury with Suquinos and Sallales as his ministers. The aerial spirits come on the South-West wind.

The seal for Michael is:

The seal for Mediat is:

The Pentacle for Mercurial Spirits is:

The Mercurial spirits provide aid in alchemy, provide metals, and facilitate transformations. They reveal information past present and future. They aid in legal matters and pacify judges, they give victory in war, aid in education and learning and teach sciences, aid in healing, raise the poor, provide wealth – though usually momentary individual sums of money not lasting wealth, cast people from honors, bind and lose spirits, open locks, aid in travel, theft, gambling, and minor oracles.

Opening

The magician has completed the pre-ritual preparations and is at the altar with his lamp lit, dimly.

The magician lights the bundle for the khernips drops it in the water and says:

Kherniptosai

The magician takes the khernips and encircles around the working space. After replacing the bowl the magician lights the four candles and then lights the incense. The magician then circles the working space with the incense and blows the incense over the altar and the tools before replacing it.

The magician touches the ground and says:

Powers of this time and place, spirits of nature be with me, make open the ways of magic and accept my thanks for your aid.

Invocation of The Divine Natural Powers

The magician raises their hands to heaven and invokes Nyx

Nyx, parent goddess, source of sweet repose,
from whom at first both Gods and men arose,
Hear, blessed Venus, deck'd with starry light,
in sleep's deep silence dwelling Ebon night!
Dreams and soft case attend thy dusky train,
pleas'd with the length'ned gloom and feastful strain.
Dissolving anxious care, the friend of Mirth,
with darkling coursers riding round the earth.
Goddess of phantoms and of shadowy play,

whose drowsy pow'r divides the nat'ral day:
By Fate's decree you constant send the light
to deepest hell, remote from mortal sight
For dire Necessity which nought withstands,
invests the world with adamantine bands.
Be present, Goddess, to thy suppliant's pray'r,
desir'd by all, whom all alike revere,
Blessed, benevolent, with friendly aid
dispell the fears of Twilight's dreadful shade.

The magician now pours wine in the offering cup for Nyx and then raises hands again to invoke Eros

I Call great Eros, source of sweet delight,
holy and pure, and lovely to the sight;
Darting, and wing'd, impetuous fierce desire,
with Gods and mortals playing, wand'ring fire:
Cautious, and two-fold, keeper of the keys
of heav'n and earth, the air, and spreading seas;
Of all that Ceres' fertile realms contains,
by which th' all-parent Goddess life sustains,
Or dismal Tartarus is doom'd to keep,
widely extended, or the sounding, deep;
For thee, all Nature's various realms obey,
who rul'st alone, with universal sway.
Come, blessed pow'r, regard these mystic fires,
and far avert, unlawful mad desires.

The magician now pours wine in the offering cup for Eros and then raises hands again to invoke Hekate

Hekate Einodia, Trioditis, lovely dame,
of earthly, watery, and celestial frame,
sepulchral, in a saffron veil arrayed,
pleased with dark ghosts that wander through the shade;
Daughter of Perses, solitary goddess, hail!
The world's key-bearer, never doomed to fail;

in stags rejoicing, huntress, nightly seen,
and drawn by bulls, unconquerable queen;
Leader, Nymphe, nurse, on mountains wandering,
hear the suppliants who with holy rites thy power revere,
and to the herdsman with a favouring mind draw near.

The magician pours wine in the offering cup for Hekate

Invocation of the Ancestors

The magician now calls upon the ancestors.

The magician knocks three times on the ancestor altar and then touches the coins

Charon, ferryman, I call upon you bring forth my ancestors and allies that you and they may partake of these offerings and they may aid me in this magic. I call upon Hades and Persephone to bring forth my ancestors and strengthen them and partake with them of these offerings.

The magician lights frankincense and myrrh and says:

I give this that the world may be made sweet for you, that through frankincense you remember that you are holy and through myrrh you find strength in death

The magician lights the two candles for the unnamed dead saying

For those ancestors by blood not named, and those ancestors not by blood not named

The magician lights the remaining candles naming each respective ancestor

The magician now briefly thanks the ancestors and explains the intention for the day

The Elementals (Optional)

Should the magician choose to call upon the aid of the elementals the appropriate elemental prayer may be inserted here.

Invocation of the Lamp

The magician places the coin, the magnet, and the wood in the scrying bowl, and traces a circle around the space with the incense, the magician then places the red cloth upon their head

The magician makes this prayer to call upon their angel while focused upon the lamp, the magician turns up the lamp's light.

Hail serpent and stout lion, natural sources of fire
Hail clear water and lofty-leafed tree
And you who gather up clover from golden fields of beans
And who cause gentle foam to gush forth from pure mouths.
Scarab who drive the orb of fertile fire,
O self-engendered one
Because you are Two-syllabled, AE,
and are the first appearing one
Nod me assent I pray, because your mystic symbols I declare,
EO AI OY AMERR OOUOTH IYIOE MARMARAUOTH
LAILAM SOUMARTA
Be gracious unto me first-father and May you yourself send strength as my companion.
Stay allied, lord, and listen to me, through the charm that produces the vision, which I [NAME] do today IY EYE OO AEE IAEE AIAE E AI EY EIE OOOOO EY EO IAOAI

I call upon you, the living god, fiery, invisible, begetter or light IAEL PEIPTA PHOS ZA PAI PHTHENTHA PHOSZA PYRI BELIA IAO IAO EYO OEE A OY EOI A E E I O Y O

give me strength, rouse your daimon, enter into this fire, fill it with a divine spirit and show me your might. Let there be opened for me the house of the all-powerful god ALBALAL who is in this light. Let there be light, breadth, depth, length, height, brightness, and let him who is inside shine through, the lord BOUEL PHTHA PHTHA PHTHAEL PHTHA ABAI BAINCHOOOCH, now now immediately, immediately, quickly, quickly.

I conjure you holy light, holy brightness, by the wholy names which I have spoken and am now going to speak. By IAO SABAOTH ARBATHIAO SESENGENBARPHARAGGES ABLANATHANALBA ALRAMMACHAMARI AI AI IAO AX AX INAX remain by me in this present hour, until, I pray to the god, and learn about the things I desire.

The magician whispers these names into the scrying bowl:

Atzam, Tzoalakoum, Geamai, Satzyne, Kalesaines, Ton, Tapesmas, Taphydou, Elylpe, Syltan, Gialoti, Mpalontzem, Thara, Pakhakhesesan, Sylbakhama, Mousamoukhana, Araga, Rhasai, Rhagana, Obras, Ouboragoras, Tzoupa, Biapophkha, Tambalakhakem, Parakhematzoum, Tou, Itana, Baphoutia, Pakhakhe, Tanretokous, Nastratie, Parakhematzoum, Tou, Itana, Baphoutia, Pakhakhe, Tanretokous, Nastratie, Pakhakhyelea, Tybalotze, Enkaika, Parpara, Oumebras, Khematzoum

Conjuration of the Angel

The magician holds the wand and the vessel of oil and conjures the angel

Hermes, draw near, and to my prayer incline,
Messenger of Jove, and Maia's son divine;
Studious of contests, ruler of mankind,
With heart almighty, and a prudent mind.

Celestial messenger, of various skill,
Whose powerful arts could watchful Argus kill:
With winged feet, through air you course,
O friend of man, and prophet of discourse:
Great life-supporter, to rejoice is thine,
In arts gymnastic, and in fraud divine:
With power endued all language to explain,
Of care the loosener, and the source of gain.
Whose hand contains of blameless peace the rod,
Corucian, blessed, profitable God;
Of various speech, whose aid in works we find,
And in necessities to mortals kind:

I conjure and call upon you, you strong and holy angels, good and powerful, in a strong name of fear and praise, Yah, Adonai, Elohim, Shaddai, Shaddai, Shaddai; Eheieh, Eheieh, Eheieh; Asamie, Asamie; and in the name of Adonai, the God of Israel, who has made the two great lights, and distinguished day from night for the benefit of his creatures; and by the names of all the discerning angels, governing openly in the second house before the great angel, Tetra, strong and powerful; and by the name of his star which is Mercury; and by the name of his seal, which is that of a powerful and honored God; I call upon you, Michael, and by the names above mentioned, Oh great angel who presides over the fourth day: and by the holy name which is written in the front of Aaron, created the most high priest, and by the names of all the angels who are constant in the grace of Christ, and by the name and place of Ammaluim, that you assist me in my labors!

The magician pours the oil into the water within the scrying bowl and commands the angel to appear in the vessel.

At this point the magician may ask the angel for needed information or make a request of the angel.

Conjuration of the Aerial Spirits (Optional)

Should the magician desire to call upon the aerial spirits the magician requests the assistance of the angel in doing so then while holding the wand and the pentacle makes this conjuration.

I conjure you Oh Mighty and potent Prince Mediat who rules as king in the dominion of the South-West. I conjure you Mediat in the name of Michael that you appear swiftly and in pleasing form with all your attending ministers in this vessel and fulfill all the things I ask of you.

This conjuration is recited until the spirit and his ministers arrive. When they arrive the magician must show them the seal of the King and the Pentacle of Solomon and say:

Behold the Pentacle of Solomon which I have brought before your presence! Behold the exorcist in this rite of the exorcism, who is who is fortified by the providence of the Most High God, fearlessly he has called you by the powerful force of this exorcism. Therefore come quickly by the virtue of these names, Aye, Saraye, Aye, Saraye, Aye, Saraye, do not delay to come, by the name of the True Eternal and Living God, Eloy, Archima, Rabur, and through this Pentacle which has been presented and powerfully rules over you and through the virtue of the Heavenly Spirits, of your Lords, and by the person of the Exorcist who has conjured you, come quickly and obediently to your master who is called Octinomos.

After calling the aerial spirits and making your petitions end the ceremony by issuing the license to depart.

License to Depart

+In the name of the Father + the Son + and the Holy Spirit go now in peace to your dwelling and let there be peace between us so that you may be ready to come again when called.

Spirits and Powers of the Sphere of Jupiter

The archangel of Jupiter is Sachiel. Suth is the king of the aerial spirits of Jupiter with Maguth and Gutrix as his ministers. The aerial spirits come on the South wind.

The seal for Sachiel is:

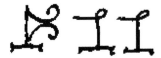

The seal for Suth is:

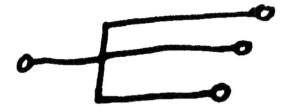

The Pentacle for Jovial Spirits is:

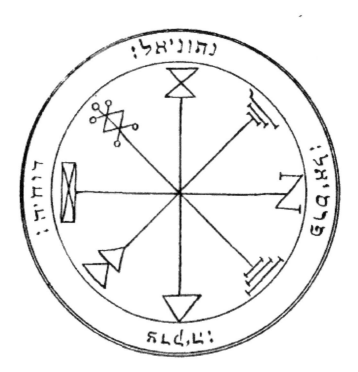

The Spirits of Jupiter bring merriment and joy, they aid in operations of love, they pacify disagreements and appease enemies, they aid in healing and conferring disease, they can cause loss or prevent loss, they promote fecundity and fertility and aid in providing lasting wealth, employment, and security.

Opening

The magician has completed the pre-ritual preparations and is at the altar with his lamp lit, dimly.

The magician lights the bundle for the khernips drops it in the water and says:

Kherniptosai

The magician takes the khernips and encircles around the working space. After replacing the bowl the magician lights the four candles and then lights the incense. The magician then circles the working space with the incense and blows the incense over the altar and the tools before replacing it.

The magician touches the ground and says:

Powers of this time and place, spirits of nature be with me, make open the ways of magic and accept my thanks for your aid.

Invocation of The Divine Natural Powers

The magician raises their hands to heaven and invokes Nyx

Nyx, parent goddess, source of sweet repose,
from whom at first both Gods and men arose,
Hear, blessed Venus, deck'd with starry light,
in sleep's deep silence dwelling Ebon night!
Dreams and soft case attend thy dusky train,
pleas'd with the length'ned gloom and feastful strain.
Dissolving anxious care, the friend of Mirth,
with darkling coursers riding round the earth.
Goddess of phantoms and of shadowy play,
whose drowsy pow'r divides the nat'ral day:

<u>Luminarium</u>

By Fate's decree you constant send the light
to deepest hell, remote from mortal sight
For dire Necessity which nought withstands,
invests the world with adamantine bands.
Be present, Goddess, to thy suppliant's pray'r,
desir'd by all, whom all alike revere,
Blessed, benevolent, with friendly aid
dispell the fears of Twilight's dreadful shade.

The magician now pours wine in the offering cup for Nyx and then raises hands again to invoke Eros

I Call great Eros, source of sweet delight,
holy and pure, and lovely to the sight;
Darting, and wing'd, impetuous fierce desire,
with Gods and mortals playing, wand'ring fire:
Cautious, and two-fold, keeper of the keys
of heav'n and earth, the air, and spreading seas;
Of all that Ceres' fertile realms contains,
by which th' all-parent Goddess life sustains,
Or dismal Tartarus is doom'd to keep,
widely extended, or the sounding, deep;
For thee, all Nature's various realms obey,
who rul'st alone, with universal sway.
Come, blessed pow'r, regard these mystic fires,
and far avert, unlawful mad desires.

The magician now pours wine in the offering cup for Eros and then raises hands again to invoke Hekate

Hekate Einodia, Trioditis, lovely dame,
of earthly, watery, and celestial frame,
sepulchral, in a saffron veil arrayed,
pleased with dark ghosts that wander through the shade;
Daughter of Perses, solitary goddess, hail!
The world's key-bearer, never doomed to fail;
in stags rejoicing, huntress, nightly seen,

and drawn by bulls, unconquerable queen;
Leader, Nymphe, nurse, on mountains wandering,
hear the suppliants who with holy rites thy power revere,
and to the herdsman with a favouring mind draw near.

The magician pours wine in the offering cup for Hekate

Invocation of the Ancestors

The magician now calls upon the ancestors.

The magician knocks three times on the ancestor altar and then touches the coins

Charon, ferryman, I call upon you bring forth my ancestors and allies that you and they may partake of these offerings and they may aid me in this magic. I call upon Hades and Persephone to bring forth my ancestors and strengthen them and partake with them of these offerings.

The magician lights frankincense and myrrh and says:

I give this that the world may be made sweet for you, that through frankincense you remember that you are holy and through myrrh you find strength in death

The magician lights the two candles for the unnamed dead saying

For those ancestors by blood not named, and those ancestors not by blood not named

The magician lights the remaining candles naming each respective ancestor

The magician now briefly thanks the ancestors and explains the intention for the day

The Elementals (Optional)

Should the magician choose to call upon the aid of the elementals the appropriate elemental prayer may be inserted here.

Invocation of the Lamp

The magician places the coin, the magnet, and the wood in the scrying bowl, and traces a circle around the space with the incense, the magician then places the red cloth upon their head

The magician makes this prayer to call upon their angel while focused upon the lamp, the magician turns up the lamp's light.

Hail serpent and stout lion, natural sources of fire
Hail clear water and lofty-leafed tree
And you who gather up clover from golden fields of beans
And who cause gentle foam to gush forth from pure mouths.
Scarab who drive the orb of fertile fire,
O self-engendered one
Because you are Two-syllabled, AE,
and are the first appearing one
Nod me assent I pray, because your mystic symbols I declare,
EO AI OY AMERR OOUOTH IYIOE MARMARAUOTH LAILAM SOUMARTA
Be gracious unto me first-father and May you yourself send strength as my companion.
Stay allied, lord, and listen to me, through the charm that produces the vision, which I [NAME] do today IY EYE OO AEE IAEE AIAE E AI EY EIE OOOOO EY EO IAOAI

I call upon you, the living god, fiery, invisible, begetter or light IAEL PEIPTA PHOS ZA PAI PHTHENTHA PHOSZA PYRI BELIA IAO IAO EYO OEE A OY EOI A E E I O Y O give me strength, rouse your daimon, enter into this fire, fill

it with a divine spirit and show me your might. Let there be opened for me the house of the all-powerful god ALBALAL who is in this light. Let there be light, breadth, depth, length, height, brightness, and let him who is inside shine through, the lord BOUEL PHTHA PHTHA PHTHAEL PHTHA ABAI BAINCHOOOCH, now now immediately, immediately, quickly, quickly.

I conjure you holy light, holy brightness, by the wholy names which I have spoken and am now going to speak. By IAO SABAOTH ARBATHIAO SESENGENBARPHARAGGES ABLANATHANALBA ALRAMMACHAMARI AI AI IAO AX AX INAX remain by me in this present hour, until, I pray to the god, and learn about the things I desire.

The magician whispers these names into the scrying bowl:

Atzam, Tzoalakoum, Geamai, Satzyne, Kalesaines, Ton, Tapesmas, Taphydou, Elylpe, Syltan, Gialoti, Mpalontzem, Thara, Pakhakhesesan, Sylbakhama, Mousamoukhana, Araga, Rhasai, Rhagana, Obras, Ouboragoras, Tzoupa, Biapophkha, Tambalakhakem, Parakhematzoum, Tou, Itana, Baphoutia, Pakhakhe, Tanretokous, Nastratie, Parakhematzoum, Tou, Itana, Baphoutia, Pakhakhe, Tanretokous, Nastratie, Pakhakhyelea, Tybalotze, Enkaika, Parpara, Oumebras, Khematzoum

Conjuration of the Angel

The magician holds the wand and the vessel of oil and conjures the angel

*O Jove much-honored, Jove supremely great,
To you our holy rites we consecrate,
Our prayers and expiations, king divine,
For all things round thy head exalted shine.
The earth is thine, and mountains swelling high,*

The sea profound, and all within the sky.
Saturnian king, descending from above,
Magnanimous, commanding, sceptered Jove;
All-parent, principle and end of all,
Whose power almighty, shakes this earthly ball;
Even Nature trembles at thy mighty nod,
Loud-sounding, armed with lightning, thundering God.
Source of abundance, purifying king,
O various-formed from whom all natures spring;
Propitious hear my prayer, give blameless health,
With peace divine, and necessary wealth.

I conjure and confirm upon you, you strong and holy angels, by the names Kadosh, Kadosh, Kadosh, Eschercie, Escherei, Eschercie, Hatim, Ya, strong founder of the worlds; Cantine, Jaym, Janic, Anic, Calbot, Sabbac, Berisay, Alnaym; and by the name Adonai, who created fishes and creeping things in the waters, and birds upon the face of the earth, flying towards heaven, in the fifth day; and by the names of the angels serving in the sixth host before Pastor, a holy angel, and a great and powerful prince and by the name of his star, which is Jupiter, and by the name of his seal, and by the name of Adonai, the great God, Creator of all things, and by the name of all the stars, and by their power and virtue, and by all the names aforesaid, I conjure thee, Sachiel, a great Angel, who is chief ruler of Thursday, that for me you will labor!

The magician pours the oil into the water within the scrying bowl and commands the angel to appear in the vessel.

At this point the magician may ask the angel for needed information or make a request of the angel.

Conjuration of the Aerial Spirits (Optional)

Should the magician desire to call upon the aerial spirits the magician requests the assistance of the angel in doing so then while holding the wand and the pentacle makes this conjuration.

I conjure you Oh Mighty and potent Prince Suth who rules as king in the dominion of the South. I conjure you Suth in the name of Sachiel that you appear swiftly and in pleasing form with all your attending ministers in this vessel and fulfill all the things I ask of you.

This conjuration is recited until the spirit and his ministers arrive. When they arrive the magician must show them the seal of the King and the Pentacle of Solomon and say:

Behold the Pentacle of Solomon which I have brought before your presence! Behold the exorcist in this rite of the exorcism, who is who is fortified by the providence of the Most High God, fearlessly he has called you by the powerful force of this exorcism. Therefore come quickly by the virtue of these names, Aye, Saraye, Aye, Saraye, Aye, Saraye, do not delay to come, by the name of the True Eternal and Living God, Eloy, Archima, Rabur, and through this Pentacle which has been presented and powerfully rules over you and through the virtue of the Heavenly Spirits, of your Lords, and by the person of the Exorcist who has conjured you, come quickly and obediently to your master who is called Octinomos.

After calling the aerial spirits and making your petitions end the ceremony by issuing the license to depart.

License to Depart

+In the name of the Father + the Son + and the Holy Spirit

go now in peace to your dwelling and let there be peace between us so that you may be ready to come again when called.

Spirits and Powers of the Sphere of Venus

The archangel of Venus is Haniel. Sarabotes is the king of the aerial spirits of Venus with Amabiel, Aba, Abalidoth, and Flaef as his ministers. The aerial spirits come on the West wind.

The seal for Haniel is:

The seal for Sarabotes is:

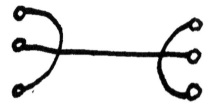

The Pentacle for Venerial Spirits is:

The Spirits of Venus excite the senses and incline people towards luxury, they may use luxury to reconcile enemies, they create marriages and partnerships, they create beauty and attraction, they create love and affection, they can create or take away illness, they provide victories, they aid in legal issues.

<u>Luminarium</u>

<u>Opening</u>

The magician has completed the pre-ritual preparations and is at the altar with his lamp lit, dimly.

The magician lights the bundle for the khernips drops it in the water and says:

Kherniptosai

The magician takes the khernips and encircles around the working space. After replacing the bowl the magician lights the four candles and then lights the incense. The magician then circles the working space with the incense and blows the incense over the altar and the tools before replacing it.

The magician touches the ground and says:

Powers of this time and place, spirits of nature be with me, make open the ways of magic and accept my thanks for your aid.

<u>Invocation of The Divine Natural Powers</u>

The magician raises their hands to heaven and invokes Nyx

Nyx, parent goddess, source of sweet repose,
from whom at first both Gods and men arose,
Hear, blessed Venus, deck'd with starry light,
in sleep's deep silence dwelling Ebon night!
Dreams and soft case attend thy dusky train,
pleas'd with the length'ned gloom and feastful strain.
Dissolving anxious care, the friend of Mirth,
with darkling coursers riding round the earth.
Goddess of phantoms and of shadowy play,

whose drowsy pow'r divides the nat'ral day:
By Fate's decree you constant send the light
to deepest hell, remote from mortal sight
For dire Necessity which nought withstands,
invests the world with adamantine bands.
Be present, Goddess, to thy suppliant's pray'r,
desir'd by all, whom all alike revere,
Blessed, benevolent, with friendly aid
dispell the fears of Twilight's dreadful shade.

The magician now pours wine in the offering cup for Nyx and then raises hands again to invoke Eros

I Call great Eros, source of sweet delight,
holy and pure, and lovely to the sight;
Darting, and wing'd, impetuous fierce desire,
with Gods and mortals playing, wand'ring fire:
Cautious, and two-fold, keeper of the keys
of heav'n and earth, the air, and spreading seas;
Of all that Ceres' fertile realms contains,
by which th' all-parent Goddess life sustains,
Or dismal Tartarus is doom'd to keep,
widely extended, or the sounding, deep;
For thee, all Nature's various realms obey,
who rul'st alone, with universal sway.
Come, blessed pow'r, regard these mystic fires,
and far avert, unlawful mad desires.

The magician now pours wine in the offering cup for Eros and then raises hands again to invoke Hekate

Hekate Einodia, Trioditis, lovely dame,
of earthly, watery, and celestial frame,
sepulchral, in a saffron veil arrayed,
pleased with dark ghosts that wander through the shade;
Daughter of Perses, solitary goddess, hail!
The world's key-bearer, never doomed to fail;

in stags rejoicing, huntress, nightly seen,
and drawn by bulls, unconquerable queen;
Leader, Nymphe, nurse, on mountains wandering,
hear the suppliants who with holy rites thy power revere,
and to the herdsman with a favouring mind draw near.

The magician pours wine in the offering cup for Hekate

Invocation of the Ancestors

The magician now calls upon the ancestors.

The magician knocks three times on the ancestor altar and then touches the coins

Charon, ferryman, I call upon you bring forth my ancestors and allies that you and they may partake of these offerings and they may aid me in this magic. I call upon Hades and Persephone to bring forth my ancestors and strengthen them and partake with them of these offerings.

The magician lights frankincense and myrrh and says:

I give this that the world may be made sweet for you, that through frankincense you remember that you are holy and through myrrh you find strength in death

The magician lights the two candles for the unnamed dead saying

For those ancestors by blood not named, and those ancestors not by blood not named

The magician lights the remaining candles naming each respective ancestor

The magician now briefly thanks the ancestors and explains the intention for the day

The Elementals (Optional)

Should the magician choose to call upon the aid of the elementals the appropriate elemental prayer may be inserted here.

Invocation of the Lamp

The magician places the coin, the magnet, and the wood in the scrying bowl, and traces a circle around the space with the incense, the magician then places the red cloth upon their head

The magician makes this prayer to call upon their angel while focused upon the lamp, the magician turns up the lamp's light.

Hail serpent and stout lion, natural sources of fire
Hail clear water and lofty-leafed tree
And you who gather up clover from golden fields of beans
And who cause gentle foam to gush forth from pure mouths.
Scarab who drive the orb of fertile fire,
O self-engendered one
Because you are Two-syllabled, AE,
and are the first appearing one
Nod me assent I pray, because your mystic symbols I declare,
EO AI OY AMERR OOUOTH IYIOE MARMARAUOTH
LAILAM SOUMARTA
Be gracious unto me first-father and May you yourself send strength as my companion.
Stay allied, lord, and listen to me, through the charm that produces the vision, which I [NAME] do today IY EYE OO AEE IAEE AIAE E AI EY EIE OOOOO EY EO IAOAI

I call upon you, the living god, fiery, invisible, begetter or light IAEL PEIPTA PHOS ZA PAI PHTHENTHA PHOSZA PYRI BELIA IAO IAO EYO OEE A OY EOI A E E I O Y O

give me strength, rouse your daimon, enter into this fire, fill it with a divine spirit and show me your might. Let there be opened for me the house of the all-powerful god ALBALAL who is in this light. Let there be light, breadth, depth, length, height, brightness, and let him who is inside shine through, the lord BOUEL PHTHA PHTHA PHTHAEL PHTHA ABAI BAINCHOOOCH, now now immediately, immediately, quickly, quickly.

I conjure you holy light, holy brightness, by the wholy names which I have spoken and am now going to speak. By IAO SABAOTH ARBATHIAO SESENGENBARPHARAGGES ABLANATHANALBA ALRAMMACHAMARI AI AI IAO AX AX INAX remain by me in this present hour, until, I pray to the god, and learn about the things I desire.

The magician whispers these names into the scrying bowl:

Atzam, Tzoalakoum, Geamai, Satzyne, Kalesaines, Ton, Tapesmas, Taphydou, Elylpe, Syltan, Gialoti, Mpalontzem, Thara, Pakhakhesesan, Sylbakhama, Mousamoukhana, Araga, Rhasai, Rhagana, Obras, Ouboragoras, Tzoupa, Biapophkha, Tambalakhakem, Parakhematzoum, Tou, Itana, Baphoutia, Pakhakhe, Tanretokous, Nastratie, Parakhematzoum, Tou, Itana, Baphoutia, Pakhakhe, Tanretokous, Nastratie, Pakhakhyelea, Tybalotze, Enkaika, Parpara, Oumebras, Khematzoum

<u>Conjuration of the Angel</u>

The magician holds the wand and the vessel of oil and conjures the angel

Heavenly, illustrious, laughter-loving queen,
Sea-born, night-loving, of an awful mien;
Crafty, from whom necessity first came,
Producing, nightly, all-connecting dame:

Yours is the world with harmony to join,
For all things spring from you, O power divine.
The triple Fates are ruled by thy decree,
And all productions yield alike to you:
Whatever the heavens, encircling all contain,
Earth fruit-producing, and the stormy main,
Your sway confesses, and obeys thy nod,
Awful attendant of the wintry God:
Goddess of marriage, charming to the sight,
Mother of Loves, whom banquets delight;
Source of persuasion, secret, favoring queen,
Illustrious born, apparent and unseen:
Spousal, lupercal, and to men inclined,
Prolific, most desired, life-giving, kind:
Great scepter bearer of the Gods, 'tis thine,
Mortals in necessary bands to join;
And every tribe of savage monsters dire
In magic chains to bind, through mad desire.
Come, Cyprus-born, and to my prayer incline,
Whether exalted in the heavens you shine,
Or pleased in Syria's temple to preside,
Or over the Egyptian plains your car to guide,
Fashioned of gold; and near its sacred flood,
Fertile and famed to fix thy blessed abode;
Or if rejoicing in the azure shores,
Near where the sea with foaming billows roars,
The circling choirs of mortals, thy delight,
Or beauteous nymphs, with eyes cerulean bright,
Pleased by the dusty banks renowned of old,
To drive your rapid, two yoked car of gold;
Or if in Cyprus with thy mother fair,
Where married females praise you every year,
And beauteous virgins in the chorus join,
Adonis pure to sing and you divine;
Come, all-attractive to my prayer inclined,
For thee, I call, with holy, reverent mind.

I conjure and confirm upon you, you strong and holy angels, by the names On, Hey, Heyah, Yah, Yah, Shaddai, Adonai, and in the name Shaddai, who created four-footed beasts, and creeping things, and man, in the sixth day, and gave to Adam power over all creatures; wherefore blessed be the name of the Creator in his place; and by the name of the angels serving in the third host, before Dagiel, a great angel, and a strong and powerful prince, and by the name of his star, which is Venus, and by his seal which is holy; and by all the names aforesaid, I conjure you, Haniel, who is the chief ruler this day, that you will labor for me!

The magician pours the oil into the water within the scrying bowl and commands the angel to appear in the vessel.

At this point the magician may ask the angel for needed information or make a request of the angel.

Conjuration of the Aerial Spirits (Optional)

Should the magician desire to call upon the aerial spirits the magician requests the assistance of the angel in doing so then while holding the wand and the pentacle makes this conjuration.

I conjure you Oh Mighty and potent Prince Sarabotes who rules as king in the dominion of the West. I conjure you Sarabotes in the name of Haniel that you appear swiftly and in pleasing form with all your attending ministers in this vessel and fulfill all the things I ask of you.

This conjuration is recited until the spirit and his ministers arrive. When they arrive the magician must show them the seal of the King and the Pentacle of Solomon and say:

Behold the Pentacle of Solomon which I have brought before your presence! Behold the exorcist in this rite of the exorcism, who is who is fortified by the providence of the Most High God, fearlessly he has called you by the powerful force of this exorcism. Therefore come quickly by the virtue of these names, Aye, Saraye, Aye, Saraye, Aye, Saraye, do not delay to come, by the name of the True Eternal and Living God, Eloy, Archima, Rabur, and through this Pentacle which has been presented and powerfully rules over you and through the virtue of the Heavenly Spirits, of your Lords, and by the person of the Exorcist who has conjured you, come quickly and obediently to your master who is called Octinomos.

After calling the aerial spirits and making your petitions end the ceremony by issuing the license to depart.

License to Depart

+In the name of the Father + the Son + and the Holy Spirit go now in peace to your dwelling and let there be peace between us so that you may be ready to come again when called.

Spirits and Powers of the Sphere of Saturn

The archangel of Saturn is Cassiel. Maymon is the king of the aerial spirits of Saturn with Abumalith, Assaibi, and Balidet as his ministers. The aerial spirits come on the South-West wind.

The seal for Cassiel is:

The seal for Maymon is:

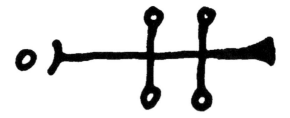

The Pentacle for Saturnine Spirits is:

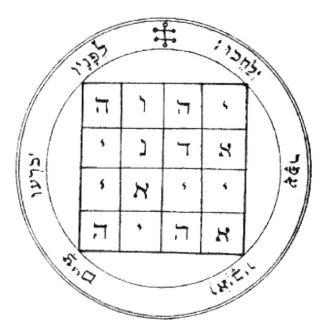

The Spirits of Saturn sow discord and hatred and create evil thoughts and agitate the mind. They may be called for operations to kill, maim or cause lameness. They confine and constrain things. They create endings and convey boundaries and the understanding of such.

<u>Luminarium</u>

Opening

The magician has completed the pre-ritual preparations and is at the altar with his lamp lit, dimly.

The magician lights the bundle for the khernips drops it in the water and says:

Kherniptosai

The magician takes the khernips and encircles around the working space. After replacing the bowl the magician lights the four candles and then lights the incense. The magician then circles the working space with the incense and blows the incense over the altar and the tools before replacing it.

The magician touches the ground and says:

Powers of this time and place, spirits of nature be with me, make open the ways of magic and accept my thanks for your aid.

Invocation of The Divine Natural Powers

The magician raises their hands to heaven and invokes Nyx

Nyx, parent goddess, source of sweet repose,
from whom at first both Gods and men arose,
Hear, blessed Venus, deck'd with starry light,
in sleep's deep silence dwelling Ebon night!
Dreams and soft case attend thy dusky train,
pleas'd with the length'ned gloom and feastful strain.
Dissolving anxious care, the friend of Mirth,
with darkling coursers riding round the earth.
Goddess of phantoms and of shadowy play,
whose drowsy pow'r divides the nat'ral day:
By Fate's decree you constant send the light

to deepest hell, remote from mortal sight
For dire Necessity which nought withstands,
invests the world with adamantine bands.
Be present, Goddess, to thy suppliant's pray'r,
desir'd by all, whom all alike revere,
Blessed, benevolent, with friendly aid
dispell the fears of Twilight's dreadful shade.

The magician now pours wine in the offering cup for Nyx and then raises hands again to invoke Eros

I Call great Eros, source of sweet delight,
holy and pure, and lovely to the sight;
Darting, and wing'd, impetuous fierce desire,
with Gods and mortals playing, wand'ring fire:
Cautious, and two-fold, keeper of the keys
of heav'n and earth, the air, and spreading seas;
Of all that Ceres' fertile realms contains,
by which th' all-parent Goddess life sustains,
Or dismal Tartarus is doom'd to keep,
widely extended, or the sounding, deep;
For thee, all Nature's various realms obey,
who rul'st alone, with universal sway.
Come, blessed pow'r, regard these mystic fires,
and far avert, unlawful mad desires.

The magician now pours wine in the offering cup for Eros and then raises hands again to invoke Hekate

Hekate Einodia, Trioditis, lovely dame,
of earthly, watery, and celestial frame,
sepulchral, in a saffron veil arrayed,
pleased with dark ghosts that wander through the shade;
Daughter of Perses, solitary goddess, hail!
The world's key-bearer, never doomed to fail;
in stags rejoicing, huntress, nightly seen,
and drawn by bulls, unconquerable queen;

*Leader, Nymphe, nurse, on mountains wandering,
hear the suppliants who with holy rites thy power revere,
and to the herdsman with a favouring mind draw near.*

The magician pours wine in the offering cup for Hekate

Invocation of the Ancestors

The magician now calls upon the ancestors.

The magician knocks three times on the ancestor altar and then touches the coins

Charon, ferryman, I call upon you bring forth my ancestors and allies that you and they may partake of these offerings and they may aid me in this magic. I call upon Hades and Persephone to bring forth my ancestors and strengthen them and partake with them of these offerings.

The magician lights frankincense and myrrh and says:

I give this that the world may be made sweet for you, that through frankincense you remember that you are holy and through myrrh you find strength in death

The magician lights the two candles for the unnamed dead saying

For those ancestors by blood not named, and those ancestors not by blood not named

The magician lights the remaining candles naming each respective ancestor

The magician now briefly thanks the ancestors and explains the intention for the day

The Elementals (Optional)

Should the magician choose to call upon the aid of the elementals the appropriate elemental prayer may be inserted here.

Invocation of the Lamp

The magician places the coin, the magnet, and the wood in the scrying bowl, and traces a circle around the space with the incense, the magician then places the red cloth upon their head

The magician makes this prayer to call upon their angel while focused upon the lamp, the magician turns up the lamp's light.

Hail serpent and stout lion, natural sources of fire
Hail clear water and lofty-leafed tree
And you who gather up clover from golden fields of beans
And who cause gentle foam to gush forth from pure mouths.
Scarab who drive the orb of fertile fire,
O self-engendered one
Because you are Two-syllabled, AE,
and are the first appearing one
Nod me assent I pray, because your mystic symbols I declare,
EO AI OY AMERR OOUOTH IYIOE MARMARAUOTH LAILAM SOUMARTA
Be gracious unto me first-father and May you yourself send strength as my companion.
Stay allied, lord, and listen to me, through the charm that produces the vision, which I [NAME] do today IY EYE OO AEE IAEE AIAE E AI EY EIE OOOOO EY EO IAOAI

I call upon you, the living god, fiery, invisible, begetter or light IAEL PEIPTA PHOS ZA PAI PHTHENTHA PHOSZA PYRI BELIA IAO IAO EYO OEE A OY EOI A E E I O Y O give me strength, rouse your daimon, enter into this fire, fill it with a divine spirit and show me your might. Let there be

opened for me the house of the all-powerful god ALBALAL who is in this light. Let there be light, breadth, depth, length, height, brightness, and let him who is inside shine through, the lord BOUEL PHTHA PHTHA PHTHAEL PHTHA ABAI BAINCHOOOCH, now now immediately, immediately, quickly, quickly.

I conjure you holy light, holy brightness, by the wholy names which I have spoken and am now going to speak. By IAO SABAOTH ARBATHIAO SESENGENBARPHARAGGES ABLANATHANALBA ALRAMMACHAMARI AI AI IAO AX AX INAX remain by me in this present hour, until, I pray to the god, and learn about the things I desire.

The magician whispers these names into the scrying bowl:

Atzam, Tzoalakoum, Geamai, Satzyne, Kalesaines, Ton, Tapesmas, Taphydou, Elylpe, Syltan, Gialoti, Mpalontzem, Thara, Pakhakhesesan, Sylbakhama, Mousamoukhana, Araga, Rhasai, Rhagana, Obras, Ouboragoras, Tzoupa, Biapophkha, Tambalakhakem, Parakhematzoum, Tou, Itana, Baphoutia, Pakhakhe, Tanretokous, Nastratie, Parakhematzoum, Tou, Itana, Baphoutia, Pakhakhe, Tanretokous, Nastratie, Pakhakhyelea, Tybalotze, Enkaika, Parpara, Oumebras, Khematzoum

Conjuration of the Angel

The magician holds the wand and the vessel of oil and conjures the angel

Etherial father, mighty Titan, hear,
Great fire of Gods and men, whom all revere:
Endued with various council, pure and strong,
To whom perfection and decrease belong.
Consumed by you all forms that hourly die,
By you restored, their former place supply;

The world immense in everlasting chains,
Strong and ineffable your power contains
Father of vast eternity, divine,
O mighty Saturn, various speech is thine:
Blossom of earth and of the starry skies,
Husband of Rhea, and Prometheus wife.
Obstetric Nature, venerable root,
From which the various forms of being shoot;
No parts peculiar can your power enclose,
Diffused through all, from which the world arose,
O, best of beings, of a subtle mind,
Propitious hear to holy prayers inclined;
The sacred rites benevolent attend,
And grant a blameless life, a blessed end.

I conjure and confirm upon you, Cassiel, Machator, and Seraquiel, strong and powerful angels; and by the name Adonai, Adonai, Adonai; Eheieh, Eheieh, Eheieh; Yehoiakim, Yehoiakim, Yehoiakim; Kadosh, Kadosh; Ima, Ima, Ima; Salay, Yah, Sar, Lord and Maker of the World, who rested on the seventh day; and by him who of his good pleasure gave the same to be observed by the children of Israel throughout their generations, that they should keep and sanctify the same, to have thereby a good reward in the world to conic; and by the names of the angels serving in the seventh host, before Booel, a great angel, and powerful prince; and by the name of his star, which is Saturn; and by his holy seal, and by the names before spoken, I conjure upon you, Cassiel, who is chief ruler of the seventh day, which is the Sabbath, that for me you will labor!

The magician pours the oil into the water within the scrying bowl and commands the angel to appear in the vessel.

At this point the magician may ask the angel for needed information or make a request of the angel.

Conjuration of the Aerial Spirits (Optional)

Should the magician desire to call upon the aerial spirits the magician requests the assistance of the angel in doing so then while holding the wand and the pentacle makes this conjuration.

I conjure you Oh Mighty and potent Prince Maymon who rules as king in the dominion of the South-West. I conjure you Maymon in the name of Cassiel that you appear swiftly and in pleasing form with all your attending ministers in this vessel and fulfill all the things I ask of you.

This conjuration is recited until the spirit and his ministers arrive. When they arrive the magician must show them the seal of the King and the Pentacle of Solomon and say:

Behold the Pentacle of Solomon which I have brought before your presence! Behold the exorcist in this rite of the exorcism, who is who is fortified by the providence of the Most High God, fearlessly he has called you by the powerful force of this exorcism. Therefore come quickly by the virtue of these names, Aye, Saraye, Aye, Saraye, Aye, Saraye, do not delay to come, by the name of the True Eternal and Living God, Eloy, Archima, Rabur, and through this Pentacle which has been presented and powerfully rules over you and through the virtue of the Heavenly Spirits, of your Lords, and by the person of the Exorcist who has conjured you, come quickly and obediently to your master who is called Octinomos.

After calling the aerial spirits and making your petitions end the ceremony by issuing the license to depart.

License to Depart

+In the name of the Father + the Son + and the Holy Spirit

go now in peace to your dwelling and let there be peace between us so that you may be ready to come again when called.

Luminarium

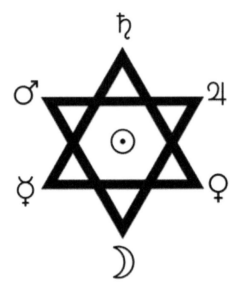

Pentacles

Pentacles are disks or tiles which have been engraved or painted with magical symbols. They are then consecrated or empowered in some fashion. Sometimes they are made simply to convey the general power of a given force, usually planetary, but sometimes elemental or zodiacal. Other times, they have special symbols to cause them to convey their powers for particular sorts of goals. The pentacles we will use are planetary and are all drawn from the S.L. MacGregor Mathers version of the Key of Solomon.

These pentacles can be consecrated, then carried or worn by the magician to gain the effects described. This is one of the traditional ways to use them. We will also present ways in the section on spells to use them in conjunction with other prayers, tools, incantations and actions for particular magical purposes.

When making one to carry or wear a paper or metal disk that can go in your wallet is often sufficient. They can be made to be worn as a necklace or kept in a special place in your bedroom.

When making them for use in spells, the material chosen will be dependent upon the spell. Sometimes they'll be on paper with something else on the other side. Sometimes you'll make it on paper large enough to burn a candle upon, or a plate big enough on which to place various spell implements. Sometimes you'll make them such that you can show them to or touch them to a person or fix them in a bag or jar of magical ingredients.

To consecrate them, you will use the ritual you used to conjure the angels. Instead of a scrying bowl you will place the pentacle being consecrated in its place. Surround the pentacle by an appropriate number of candles (Saturn, 3, Jupiter, 4, Mars, 5, Sol, 6, Venus, 7, Mercury, 8, Luna, 9). The candles should be of the appropriate color. Take a stone of the appropriate color and a magnet and place them on your pentacle. When you have called upon the angel, request that it consecrate the pentacle. As you make your request, anoint the pentacle with oil related to the magical intention for which it will be used. Then read the psalm for consecrating pentacles, and if there is a psalm appropriate to your individual pentacle, read that as well. Then finish the ritual with the license to depart. Leave the pentacle with the stone and magnet and allow the candles to burn out.

Psalm 57 *(1) Save me, O God, by thy name, and judge me by thy strength. (2) Hear my prayer, O God; give ear to the words of my mouth. (3) For strangers are risen up against me, and oppressors seek after my soul: they have not set God before them. Selah. (4) Behold, God is mine helper: the Lord is with them that uphold my soul. (5) He shall reward evil unto mine enemies: cut them off in thy truth. (6) I will freely sacrifice unto thee: I will praise thy name, O Lord; for it is good. (7) For he hath delivered me out of all trouble: and mine eye hath seen his desire upon mine enemies.*

Sol

This is the First Pentacle of the Sun and is used to command the Solar spirits. The image is of the Metatron and therefore is a face before whom all angels kneel and give reverence. The verse around it is "Behold His face and form by Whom all things were made, and Whom all creatures obey."

This is the Sixth Pentacle of the Sun; it is used for operations of invisibility. The Holy Name associated therewith is Shaddai. The psalm to be prayed during the consecration is Psalm 69.

Psalm 69 (1) Save me, O God; for the waters are come in unto my soul. (2) I sink in deep mire, where there is no standing: I am come into deep waters, where the floods overflow me. (3) I am weary of my crying: my throat is dried: mine eyes fail while I wait for my God. (4) They that hate me without a cause are more than the hairs of mine head: they that would destroy me, being mine enemies wrongfully, are mighty: then I restored that which I took not away. (5) O God, thou knowest my foolishness; and my sins are not hid from thee. (6) Let not them that wait on thee, O Lord GOD of hosts, be ashamed for my sake: let not those that seek thee be confounded for my sake, O God of Israel. (7) Because for thy sake I have borne reproach; shame hath covered my face. (8) I am become a stranger unto my brethren, and an alien unto my mother's children. (9) For the zeal of thine house hath eaten me up; and the reproaches of them that reproached thee are fallen upon me. (10) When I wept, and chastened my soul with fasting, that was to my reproach. (11) I made sackcloth also my garment; and I became a proverb to them. (12) They that sit in the gate speak against me; and I was the song of the drunkards. (13) But as for me, my prayer is unto thee, O Lord, in an acceptable time: O God, in the multitude of thy mercy hear me, in the truth of thy salvation. (14) Deliver me out of the mire, and let me not sink: let me be delivered from them that hate me, and out of the deep waters. (15) Let not the waterflood overflow me, neither let the deep swallow me up, and let not the pit shut her mouth upon me. (16) Hear me, O Lord; for thy lovingkindness is good: turn unto me according to the multitude of thy tender mercies. (17) And hide not thy face from thy servant; for I am in trouble: hear me speedily. (18) Draw nigh unto my soul, and redeem it: deliver me because of mine enemies. (19) Thou hast known my reproach, and my shame, and my dishonour: mine adversaries are all before thee. (20) Reproach hath broken my heart; and I am full of heaviness: and I looked for some to take pity, but there was none; and for comforters, but I found none. (21) They gave me also gall for my meat; and in my thirst they gave me vinegar to drink. (22) Let their table become a snare before them: and that which should have been for their welfare, let it become a trap. (23) Let their eyes be darkened, that they see not; and make their loins continually to shake. (24) Pour out thine indignation upon them, and let thy wrathful anger take hold of them. (25) Let their habitation be desolate; and let none dwell in their tents. (26) For they persecute him whom thou hast smitten; and they talk to the grief of those whom thou hast wounded. (27) Add iniquity unto their iniquity: and let them not come into thy righteousness. (28) Let them be blotted out of the book of the living, and not be written with the righteous. (29) But I am poor and sorrowful: let thy salvation, O God, set me up on high. (30) I will praise the name of God with a song, and will magnify him with thanksgiving. (31) This also shall please the Lord better than an ox or bullock that hath horns and hoofs. (32) The humble shall see this, and be glad: and your heart shall live that seek God. (33) For the Lord heareth the poor, and despiseth not his prisoners. (34) Let the heaven and earth praise him, the seas, and everything that moveth therein. (35) For God will save Zion, and will build the cities of Judah: that they may dwell there, and have it in possession. (36) The seed also of his servants shall inherit it: and they that love his name shall dwell therein.

Luna

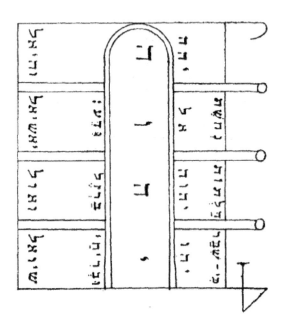

This is the First Pentacle of the Moon and it is used to call upon the Lunar Spirits. It can also be used to open doors and gateways, things which have been closed off. The seal references the divine names IHV, IHVH, AL, and IHH; it references the angels Schioel, Vaol, Yashiel, Vehiel. It is consecrated with Psalm 107.

Psalm 107 *(1) O give thanks unto the Lord, for he is good: for his mercy endureth for ever. (2) Let the redeemed of the Lord say so, whom he hath redeemed from the hand of the enemy; (3) And gathered them out of the lands, from the east, and from the west, from the north, and from the south. (4) They wandered in the wilderness in a solitary way; they found no city to dwell in. (5) Hungry and thirsty, their soul fainted in them. (6) Then they cried unto the Lord in their trouble, and he delivered them out of their distresses. (7) And he led them forth by the right way, that they might go to a city of habitation. (8) Oh that men would praise the Lord for his goodness, and for his wonderful works to the children of men! (9) For he satisfieth the longing soul, and filleth the hungry soul with goodness. (10) Such as sit in darkness and in the shadow of death, being bound in affliction and iron; (11) Because they rebelled against the words of God, and contemned the counsel of the most High: (12) Therefore he brought down their heart with labour; they fell down, and there was none to help. (13) Then they cried unto the Lord in their trouble, and he saved them out of their distresses. (14) He brought them out of darkness and the shadow of death, and brake their bands in sunder. (15) Oh that men would praise the Lord for his goodness, and for his wonderful works to the children of men! (16) For he hath broken the gates of brass, and cut the bars of iron in sunder. (17) Fools because of their transgression, and because of their iniquities, are afflicted. (18) Their soul abhorreth all manner of meat; and they draw near unto the gates of death. (19) Then they cry unto the Lord in their trouble, and he saveth them out of their distresses. (20) He sent his word, and healed them, and delivered them from their destructions. (21) Oh that men would praise the Lord for his goodness, and for his wonderful works to the children of men! (22) And let them sacrifice the sacrifices of thanksgiving, and declare his works with rejoicing. (23) They that go down to the sea in ships, that do business in great waters; (24) These see the works of the Lord, and his wonders in the deep. (25) For he commandeth, and raiseth the stormy wind, which lifteth up the waves thereof. (26) They mount up to the heaven, they go down again to the depths: their soul is melted because of trouble. (27) They reel to and fro, and stagger like a drunken man, and are at their wit's end. (28) Then they cry unto the Lord in their trouble, and he bringeth them out of their distresses. (29) He maketh the storm a calm, so that the waves thereof are still. (30) Then are they glad because they be quiet; so he bringeth them unto their desired haven. (31) Oh that men would praise the Lord for his goodness, and for his wonderful works to the children of men! (32) Let them exalt him also in the congregation of the people, and praise him in the assembly of the elders. (33) He turneth rivers into a wilderness, and the watersprings into dry ground; (34) A fruitful land into barrenness, for the wickedness of them that dwell therein. (35) He turneth the wilderness into a standing water, and dry ground into watersprings. (36) And there he maketh the hungry to dwell, that they may prepare a city for habitation; (37) And sow the fields, and plant vineyards, which may yield fruits of increase. (38) He blesseth them also, so that they are multiplied greatly; and suffereth not their cattle to decrease. (39) Again, they are minished and brought low through oppression, affliction, and sorrow. (40) He poureth contempt upon princes, and causeth them to wander in the wilderness, where there is no way. (41) Yet setteth he the poor on high from affliction, and maketh him families like a flock. (42) The righteous shall see it, and rejoice: and all iniquity shall stop her mouth. (43) Whoso is wise, and will observe these things, even they shall understand the lovingkindness of the Lord.*

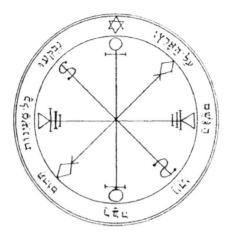

This is this Sixth Pentacle of the Moon; it is used to cause heavy rains. Traditionally this is done by engraving the seal on a silver plate and placing it under water so that the rains will continue, and they will remain as long as the seal is submerged. It is associated with the verse Genesis 7:11-12, "All the fountains of the great deep were broken up…and the rain was upon the earth."

Mars

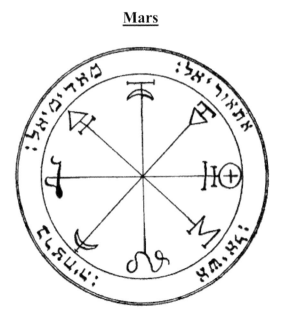

This is the First Pentacle of Mars; it is used to call upon the Martial spirits. The angels associated with this seal are Madimiel, Bartzachiah, Eschiel, and Ithuriel.

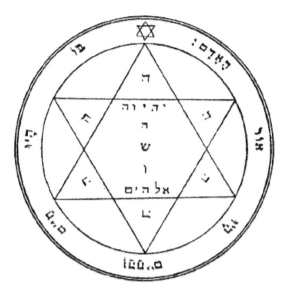

This is the Second Pentacle of Mars. It has a reputation for being very powerful both in healing and preventing illness. Associated with this pentacle is John 1:4, "In Him was life, and the life was the light of man." The pentacle, when properly consecrated, may be worn or held in close possession of the one for whom it provides protection, or touched to an ill person.

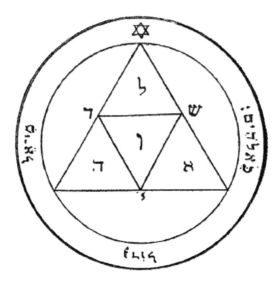

This is the Third Pentacle of Mars. It can be used for creating hostilities between people, stirring feelings of wrath or brewing war and discord. Its psalm is Psalm 127. It is associated with the Holy Names Eloah and Shaddai.

Psalm 127 *(1) Except the Lord build the house, they labour in vain that build it: except the Lord keep the city, the watchman waketh but in vain. (2) It is vain for you to rise up early, to sit up late, to eat the bread of sorrows: for so he giveth his beloved sleep. (3) Lo, children are an heritage of the Lord: and the fruit of the womb is his reward. (4) As arrows are in the hand of a mighty man; so are children of the youth. (5) Happy is the man that hath his quiver full of them: they shall not be ashamed, but they shall speak with the enemies in the gate.*

Mercury

This is the Third Pentacle of Mercury; it is used to conjure the spirits of Mercury. It is particularly associated with the angels Kokaviel, Gheoria, Savaniah, and Chokmahiel.

This is the Fifth Pentacle of Mercury and it is used to open doors, no matter how they are closed, and nothing can resist being opened by it. The Holy Names El, Ab, and IHVH are associated with this pentacle. Psalm 24 is the psalm associated with this pentacle.

Psalm 24 *(1) The earth is the Lord's, and the fulness thereof; the world, and they that dwell therein. (2) For he hath founded it upon the seas, and established it upon the floods. (3) Who shall ascend into the hill of the Lord? or who shall stand in his holy place? (4) He that hath clean hands, and a pure heart; who hath not lifted up his soul unto vanity, nor sworn deceitfully. (5) He shall receive the blessing from the Lord, and righteousness from the God of his salvation. (6) This is the generation of them that seek him, that seek thy face, O Jacob. Selah. (7) Lift up your heads, O ye gates; and be ye lift up, ye everlasting doors; and the King of glory shall come in. (8) Who is this King of glory? The Lord strong and mighty, the Lord mighty in battle. (9) Lift up your heads, O ye gates; even lift them up, ye everlasting doors; and the King of glory shall come in. (10) Who is this King of glory? The Lord of hosts, he is the King of glory. Selah.*

Jupiter

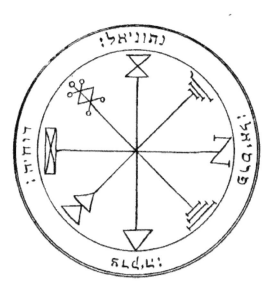

This is the First Pentacle of Jupiter it is used to invoke the Spirits of Jupiter. Parasiel, the Lord and Master of Treasures is especially associated with this pentacle and may be called upon to reveal how to possess places in which treasure is hidden. Also associated with this are the angels Netoniel, Devachiah, and Tzedeqiah.

This is the Second Pentacle of Jupiter; it aids in acquiring glory, honors, dignities, riches, mental tranquility, all sorts of goods, and helps remove spirits guarding treasure. Traditionally it is made with Virgin Parchment, written with bat or screech owl blood, but, can be made in various fashions like the rest of the pentacles. It is associated with the names AHIH, AB, and IHVH and with Psalm 112, and the verse, "Wealth and Riches are in his house and his righteousness endureth forever."

Psalm 112 *(1) Praise ye the Lord. Blessed is the man that feareth the Lord, that delighteth greatly in his commandments. (2) His seed shall be mighty upon earth: the generation of the upright shall be blessed. (3) Wealth and riches shall be in his house: and his righteousness endureth for ever. (4) Unto the upright there ariseth light in the darkness: he is gracious, and full of compassion, and righteous. (5) A good man sheweth favour, and lendeth: he will guide his affairs with discretion. (6) Surely he shall not be moved for ever: the righteous shall be in everlasting remembrance. (7) He shall not be afraid of evil tidings: his heart is fixed, trusting in the Lord. (8) His heart is established, he shall not be afraid, until he see his desire upon his enemies. (9) He hath dispersed, he hath given to the poor; his righteousness endureth for ever; his horn shall be exalted with honour. (10) The wicked shall see it, and be grieved; he shall gnash with his teeth, and melt away: the desire of the wicked shall perish.*

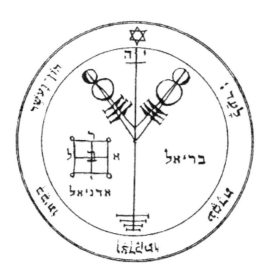

This is the Fourth Pentacle of Jupiter; it serves to acquire riches and honor and wealth. It is associated with the angel Bariel. I have conjured Bariel and used this seal to great success multiple times, with life-changing effects. The traditional instructions say to construct the pentacle out of silver and engrave it in the day and hour of Jupiter when Jupiter is in Cancer. It is effective when drawn on paper, wood or wax as well. Traditionally tin is associated with Jupiter. The seal is associated with the Holy name IH, the angels Bariel and Adoniel, and Psalm 112.

Psalm 112 *(1) Praise ye the Lord. Blessed is the man that feareth the Lord, that delighteth greatly in his commandments. (2) His seed shall be mighty upon earth: the generation of the upright shall be blessed. (3) Wealth and riches shall be in his house: and his righteousness endureth for ever. (4) Unto the upright there ariseth light in the darkness: he is gracious, and full of compassion, and righteous. (5) A good man sheweth favour, and lendeth: he will guide his affairs with discretion. (6) Surely he shall not be moved for ever: the righteous shall be in everlasting remembrance. (7) He shall not be afraid of evil tidings: his heart is fixed, trusting in the Lord. (8) His heart is established, he shall not be afraid, until he see his desire upon his enemies. (9) He hath dispersed, he hath given to the poor; his righteousness endureth for ever; his horn shall be exalted with honour. (10) The wicked shall see it, and be grieved; he shall gnash with his teeth, and melt away: the desire of the wicked shall perish.*

This is the Seventh Pentacle of Jupiter; it is powerful against poverty, especially when contemplated while repeating the verse, "Lifting up the poor out of the mire, and raising the needy from the dunghill, that he may set him with princes, even with the princes of his people." It is associated with Psalm 113.

Psalm 113 *(1) Praise ye the Lord. Praise, O ye servants of the Lord, praise the name of the Lord. (2) Blessed be the name of the Lord from this time forth and for evermore. (3) From the rising of the sun unto the going down of the same the Lord's name is to be praised. (4) The Lord is high above all nations, and his glory above the heavens. (5) Who is like unto the Lord our God, who dwelleth on high, (6) Who humbleth himself to behold the things that are in heaven, and in the earth! (7) He raiseth up the poor out of the dust, and lifteth the needy out of the dunghill; (8) That he may set him with princes, even with the princes of his people. (9) He maketh the barren woman to keep house, and to be a joyful mother of children. Praise ye the Lord.*

Venus

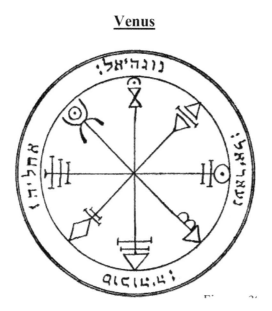

This is the First Pentacle of Venus and is used to control the Spirits of Venus, in particular those associated with the pentacle, Nogahiel, Acheliah, Socodiah, and Nangariel.

This is the Third Pentacle of Venus; showing it to someone will stir love in them. It is associated with the angel Monachiel, who can be invoked with the pentacle in the day and hour of Venus. The Holy Names IHVH, Adonai, Ruakh, Achides, are associated with the pentacle, along with the angels Aegalmiel, Monachiel, and Degaliel. It is associated with the verse Genesis 1:28, "And the Elohim blessed them and the Elohim said unto them, Be ye fruitful and multiply and replenish the earth and subdue it." I have worked with Monachiel and with this seal several times with success. Monachiel is one of the more approachable angels for operations of love.

This is the Fifth Pentacle of Venus; like the last, it excites people to love when it is shown to them. It is associated with the Holy Names Elohim, El, and Gebil, and is associated with Psalm 22. This seal is quite simple and quite powerful and I have used it in the past to great effect with little effort.

Psalm 22 *(1) My God, my God, why hast thou forsaken me? why art thou so far from helping me, and from the words of my roaring? (2) O my God, I cry in the daytime, but thou hearest not; and in the night season, and am not silent. (3) But thou art holy, O thou that inhabitest the praises of Israel. (4) Our fathers trusted in thee: they trusted, and thou didst deliver them. (5) They cried unto thee, and were delivered: they trusted in thee, and were not confounded. (6) But I am a worm, and no man; a reproach of men, and despised of the people. (7) All they that see me laugh me to scorn: they shoot out the lip, they shake the head saying, (8) He trusted on the Lord that he would deliver him: let him deliver him, seeing he delighted in him. (9) But thou art he that took me out of the womb: thou didst make me hope when I was upon my mother's breasts. (10) I was cast upon thee from the womb:*

thou art my God from my mother's belly. (11) Be not far from me; for trouble is near; for there is none to help. (12) Many bulls have compassed me: strong bulls of Bashan have beset me round. (13) They gaped upon me with their mouths, as a ravening and a roaring lion. (14) I am poured out like water, and all my bones are out of joint: my heart is like wax; it is melted in the midst of my bowels. (15) My strength is dried up like a potsherd; and my tongue cleaveth to my jaws; and thou hast brought me into the dust of death. (16) For dogs have compassed me: the assembly of the wicked have inclosed me: they pierced my hands and my feet. (17) I may tell all my bones: they look and stare upon me. (18: They part my garments among them, and cast lots upon my vesture. (19) But be not thou far from me, O Lord: O my strength, haste thee to help me. (20) Deliver my soul from the sword; my darling from the power of the dog. (21) Save me from the lion's mouth: for thou hast heard me from the horns of the unicorns. (22) I will declare thy name unto my brethren: in the midst of the congregation will I praise thee. (23) Ye that fear the Lord, praise him; all ye the seed of Jacob, glorify him; and fear him, all ye the seed of Israel. (24) For he hath not despised nor abhorred the affliction of the afflicted; neither hath he hid his face from him; but when he cried unto him, he heard. (25) My praise shall be of thee in the great congregation: I will pay my vows before them that fear him. (26) The meek shall eat and be satisfied: they shall praise the Lord that seek him: your heart shall live for ever. (27) All the ends of the world shall remember and turn unto the Lord: and all the kindreds of the nations shall worship before thee. (28) For the kingdom is the Lord's: and he is the governor among the nations. (29) All they that be fat upon earth shall eat and worship: all they that go down to the dust shall bow before him: and none can keep alive his own soul. (30) A seed shall serve him; it shall be accounted to the Lord for a generation. (31) They shall come, and shall declare his righteousness unto a people that shall be born, that he hath done this.

Saturn

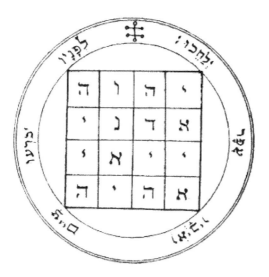

This is the First Pentacle of Saturn; it is described as being used to strike terror into spirits, and may be used when conjuring the spirits of Saturn. It is associated with the Holy Names, IHVH, ADNI, IIAI, and AHIH. It is associated with Psalm 72.

Psalm 72 *(1) Give the king thy judgments, O God, and thy righteousness unto the king's son. (2) He shall judge thy people with righteousness, and thy poor with judgment. (3) The mountains shall bring peace to the people, and the little hills, by righteousness. (4) He shall judge the poor of the people, he shall save the children of the needy, and shall break in pieces the oppressor. (5) They shall fear thee as long as the sun and moon endure, throughout all generations. (6) He shall come down like rain upon the mown grass: as showers that water the earth. (7) In his days shall the righteous flourish; and abundance of peace so long as the moon endureth. (8) He shall have dominion also from sea to sea, and from the river unto the ends of the earth. (9) They that dwell in the wilderness shall bow before him; and his enemies shall lick the dust. (10) The kings of Tarshish and of the isles shall bring presents: the kings of Sheba and Seba shall offer gifts. (11) Yea, all kings shall fall down before him: all nations shall serve him. (12) For he shall deliver the needy when he crieth; the poor also, and him that hath no helper. (13) He shall spare the poor and needy, and shall save the souls of the needy. (14) He shall redeem their soul from deceit and violence: and precious shall their blood be in his sight. (15) And he shall live, and to him shall be given of the gold of Sheba: prayer also shall be made for him continually; and daily shall he be praised. (16) There shall be an handful of corn in the earth upon the top of the mountains; the fruit thereof shall shake like Lebanon: and they of the city shall flourish like grass of the earth. (17) His name shall endure for ever: his name shall be continued as long as the sun: and men shall be blessed in him: all nations shall call him blessed. (18) Blessed be the Lord God, the God of Israel, who only doeth wondrous things. (19) And blessed be his glorious name for ever: and let the whole earth be filled with his glory; Amen, and Amen. (20) The prayers of David the son of Jesse are ended.*

The Fourth Pentacle of Saturn is used for causing ruin, destruction, and death. It can also be used to draw spirits of good news when calling spirits from the South. It is associated with Psalm 109.

Psalm 109 *(1) Hold not thy peace, O God of my praise; (2) For the mouth of the wicked and the mouth of the deceitful are opened against me: they have spoken against me with a lying tongue. (3) They compassed me about also with words of hatred; and fought against me without a cause. (4) For my love they are my adversaries: but I give myself unto prayer. (5) And they have rewarded me evil for good, and hatred for my love. (6) Set thou a wicked man over him: and let Satan stand at his right hand. (7) When he shall be judged, let him be condemned: and let his prayer become sin. (8) Let his days be few; and let another take his office. (9) Let his children be fatherless, and his wife a widow. (10) Let his children be continually vagabonds, and beg: let them seek their bread also out of their desolate places. (11) Let the extortioner catch all that he hath; and let the strangers spoil his labour. (12) Let there be none to extend mercy unto him: neither let there be any to favour his fatherless children. (13) Let his posterity be cut off; and in the generation following let their name be blotted out. (14) Let the iniquity of his fathers be remembered with the Lord; and let not the sin of his mother be blotted out. (15) Let them be before the Lord continually, that he may cut off the memory of them from the earth. (16) Because that he remembered not to shew mercy, but persecuted the poor and needy man, that he might even slay the broken in heart. (17) As he loved cursing, so let it come unto him: as he delighted not in blessing, so let it be far from him. (18) As he clothed himself with cursing like as with his garment, so let it come into his bowels like water, and like oil into his bones. (19) Let it be unto him as the garment which covereth him, and for a girdle wherewith he is girded continually. (20) Let this be the reward of mine adversaries from the Lord, and of them that speak evil against my soul. (21) But do thou for me, O God the Lord, for thy name's sake: because thy mercy is good, deliver thou me. (22) For I am poor and needy, and my heart is wounded within me. (23) I am gone like the shadow when it declineth: I am tossed up and down as the locust. (24) My knees are weak through fasting; and my flesh faileth of fatness. (25) I became also a reproach unto them: when they looked upon me they shaked their heads. (26) Help me, O Lord my God: O save me according to thy mercy: (27) That they may know that this is thy hand; that thou, Lord, hast done it. (28) Let them curse, but bless thou: when they arise, let them be ashamed; but let thy servant rejoice. (29) Let mine adversaries be clothed with shame, and let them cover themselves with their own confusion, as with a mantle. (30) I will greatly praise the Lord with my mouth; yea, I will praise him among the multitude. (31) For he shall stand at the right hand of the poor, to save him from those that condemn his soul.*

This is the Seventh Pentacle of Saturn; it is used to cause earthquakes by the might of the angels named therein, who are all mighty enough to set the earth to trembling and shaking. The pentacle lists the orders of angels: The Hayyoth, the Ophanim, the Aralim, the Chashmalim, the Seraphim, the Malakim, the Elohim, the Beni Elohim, and the Kerubim. The pentacle is associated with 18th Psalm and the verse, "Then the earth shook and trembled, the foundations of the hills also moved and were shaken, because He was wroth."

Psalm 18 *(1) I will love thee, O Lord, my strength. (2) The Lord is my rock, and my fortress, and my deliverer; my God, my strength, in whom I will trust; my buckler, and the horn of my salvation, and my high tower. (3) I will call upon the Lord, who is worthy to be praised: so shall I be saved from mine enemies. (4) The sorrows of death compassed me, and the floods of ungodly men made me afraid. (5) The sorrows of hell compassed me about: the snares of death prevented me. (6) In my distress I called upon the Lord, and cried unto my God: he heard my voice out of his temple, and my cry came before him, even into his ears. (7) Then the earth shook and trembled; the foundations also of the hills moved and were shaken, because he was wroth. (8) There went up a smoke out of his nostrils, and fire out of his mouth devoured: coals were kindled by it. (9) He bowed the heavens also, and came down: and darkness was under his feet. (10) And he rode upon a cherub, and did fly: yea, he did fly upon the wings of the wind. (11) He made darkness his secret place; his pavilion round about him were dark waters and thick clouds of the skies. (12) At the brightness that was before him his thick clouds passed, hail stones and coals of fire. (13) The Lord also thundered in the heavens, and the Highest gave his voice; hail stones and coals of fire. (14) Yea, he sent out his arrows, and scattered them; and he shot out lightnings, and discomfited them. (15) Then the channels of waters were seen, and the foundations of the world were discovered at thy rebuke, O Lord, at the blast of the breath of thy nostrils. (16) He sent from above, he took me, he drew me out of many waters. (17) He delivered me from my strong enemy, and from them which hated me: for they were too strong for me. (18) They prevented me in the day of my calamity: but the Lord was my stay. (19) He brought me forth also into a large place; he delivered me, because he delighted in me. (20) The Lord rewarded me according to my righteousness; according to the cleanness of my hands hath he recompensed me. (21) For I have kept the ways of the Lord, and have not wickedly departed from my God. (22) For all his judgments were before me, and I did not put away his statutes from me. (23) I was also upright before him, and I kept myself from mine iniquity. (24) Therefore hath the Lord recompensed me according to my righteousness, according to the cleanness of my hands in his eyesight. (25) With the merciful thou wilt shew thyself merciful; with an upright man thou wilt shew thyself upright; (26) With the pure thou wilt shew thyself pure; and with the froward thou wilt shew thyself froward. (27) For thou wilt save the afflicted people; but wilt bring down high looks. (28) For thou wilt light my candle: the Lord my God will enlighten my darkness. (29) For by thee I have run through a troop; and by my God have I leaped over a wall. (30) As for God, his way is perfect: the word of the Lord is tried: he is a buckler to all those that trust in him. (31) For who is God save the Lord? or who is a rock save our God? (32) It is God that girdeth me with strength, and maketh my way perfect. (33) He maketh my feet like hinds' feet, and setteth me upon my high places. (34) He teacheth my hands to war, so that a bow of steel is broken by mine arms. (35) Thou hast also given me the shield of thy salvation: and thy right hand hath holden me up, and thy gentleness hath made me great. (36) Thou hast enlarged my steps under me, that my feet did not slip. (37) I have pursued mine enemies, and overtaken them: neither did I turn again till they were consumed. (38) I have wounded them that they were not able to rise: they are fallen under my feet. (39) For thou hast girded me with strength unto the battle: thou hast subdued under me those that rose up against me. (40) Thou hast also given me the necks of mine enemies; that I might destroy them that hate me. (41) They cried, but there was none to save them: even unto the Lord, but he answered them not. (42) Then did I beat them small as the dust before the wind: I did cast them out as the dirt in the streets. (43) Thou hast delivered me from the strivings of the people; and thou hast made me the head of the heathen: a people whom I have not known shall serve me. (44) As soon as they hear of me, they shall obey me: the strangers shall submit themselves unto me. (45) The strangers shall fade away, and be afraid out of their close places. (46) The Lord liveth; and blessed be my rock; and let the God of my salvation be exalted. (47) It is God that avengeth me, and subdueth the people under me. (48) He delivereth me from mine enemies: yea, thou liftest me up above those that rise up against me: thou hast delivered me from the violent man. (49) Therefore will I give thanks unto thee, O Lord, among the heathen, and sing praises unto thy name. (50) Great deliverance giveth he to his king; and sheweth mercy to his anointed, to David, and to his seed for evermore.*

Luminarium

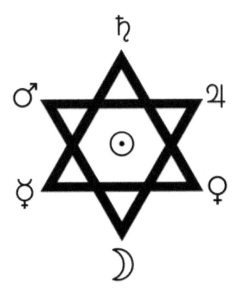

Spells

The spells we will provide combine elements from a handful of traditional sources. Many will use the pentacles provided. In some cases, the pentacle will work like a battery, or a spirit touch point for the spell. Typically, a small prayer to call upon the associated angel will be sufficient, if you have already conjured the angel and asked it to come when you call and to assist you in magic. If the angel agrees to this in the conjuration, and you fulfill whatever the terms of the agreement are, in most cases you won't need a full conjuration for these spells – but you can also run the full conjuration rather than using the simple prayer if you feel you need a more complete and powerful presence for your goal. If you have bound the aerial kings and their ministers, or if the aerial king has provided you with a familiar spirit you may call upon the angel through prayer to send the aerial spirits or you may call upon your familiar to assist with the work of the spell. If using the aerial spirits or the familiar, add the pentacle by which the spirits of that planetary sphere are compelled.

Some of these spells have been tested and have seen success. Some contain pieces which have been used successfully and are augmented or given context through the work presented here for people who may not have the magical conditions to use the components on their own. Some are experimental and have been assembled from multiple traditional components. In one case, the spell manifested its effect as I was writing it for this text. In another case, the components from various sources all tied to the same psalm without my realizing until they were finally assembled. Various other instances showed links in the choices for the less-tested examples. In all cases, these are examples of how you can combine elements of folk magic and sorcery with conjuration. You can use these examples as inspiration to build your own experiments.

Depending upon your morality, some of the spells may be morally questionable. In such cases, simply don't do the ones you find objectionable. Or don't do any and find others, or build your own. The inclusion of any given spell is not a recommendation to use it, but simply an example of the magic related to that planet.

Sol

For Invisibility

When you desire to move through a space unnoticed or undetected, use this spell.

Paint the Sixth Pentacle of the Sun upon a plate or bowl. Consecrate it in ritual.

Once you have the consecrated bowl, place six bay leaves in the bowl.

Say this prayer

Holy Father, Lord of Hosts, Most High God, Font of Mercy, send forth your light through the gracious presence of your angel Raphael. Send your good angel upon me that I may be made unseen. St. Raphael bend light and sound that I may go unnoticed. Close the eyes of those who would look upon me so that my light does not reach them. Let me pass safely as if through darkness.

Bend down so that you may whisper directly onto the bay leaves and say:

Let their eyes be darkened that they see not; and make their loins continually to shake. They have eyes and see not

Athatos itiros theon pantocraton (6x)

Let their eyes be darkened that they see not; and make their loins continually to shake. They have eyes and see not. Amen

Carry one of the leaves with you when you need to go unseen or unnoticed.

To Reunite with an Estranged Friend

If you have a friend with whom you have lost contact and would like to restore contact but are concerned that they may not be on the same page utilize this spell.

Draw this square on a piece of paper

I	A	L	D	A	H
A	Q	O	R	I	A
L	O	Q	I	R	B
D	R	I	I	D	E
A	I	R	D	R	O
H	A	F	E	O	N

On the back side of the square write your friend's name seven times then rotate 90 degrees clockwise and write your name seven times. Around the name cross-hatching, write your intention to reunite with this friend amicably, without lifting your pen from the paper so that the intention forms an unbroken circle. Say the intention aloud as you write it.

Say this prayer and anoint the paper with a 5 spot of frankincense or red sandalwood oil.

Holy Father, Lord of Hosts, Most High God, Font of Mercy, send forth your healing through the gracious presence of your angel Raphael. Send your good angel upon me that I may be made whole. St. Raphael, pray for me and for [Name of Friend] that our hearts may be whole again and we might return to each other in love and friendship. Strike down the disease which separates us and return to us the comradery we once had. In the name of the Lord of Love and Friendship, the God of Hosts, the Help of the Helpless, St. Raphael heal my heart and bring upon my desire, amen.

Dress a yellow or gold candle with rose oil and burn it over your petition so that the wax settles over the names and seals them together. While the candle is burning, pray the Orphic Hymn of the Sun.

When the wax has set, carry the talisman to an open field beneath the shining sun. Call the name of your friend and speak from the heart your desire to be reunited. Hold up the talisman in your right hand and pray Psalm 85.

Psalm 85 *(1) Lord, thou hast been favourable unto thy land: thou hast brought back the captivity of Jacob. (2) Thou hast forgiven the iniquity of thy people, thou hast covered all their sin. Selah. (3) Thou hast taken away all thy wrath: thou hast turned thyself from the fierceness of thine anger. (4) Turn us, O God of our salvation, and cause thine anger toward us to cease. (5) Wilt thou be angry with us for ever? wilt thou draw out thine anger to all generations? (6) Wilt thou not revive us again: that thy people may rejoice in thee? (7) Shew us thy mercy, O Lord, and grant us thy salvation. (8) I will hear what God the Lord will speak: for he will speak peace unto his people, and to his saints: but let them not turn again to folly. (9) Surely his salvation is nigh them that fear him; that glory may dwell in our land. (10) Mercy and truth are met together; righteousness and peace have kissed each other. (11) Truth shall spring out of the earth; and righteousness shall look down from heaven. (12) Yea, the Lord shall give that which is good; and our land shall yield her increase. (13)*

Righteousness shall go before him; and shall set us in the way of his steps.

When you see your friend wear the rose oil along with the oil with which you anointed the talisman.

Luna

To Appear Beautiful and Enchanting

Obtain a gallon of spring water. Set the spring water in an enclosed container upon the consecrated First Pentacle of the Moon; set the pentacle atop a mirror smeared with water in which mugwort has soaked, somewhere that it will catch the light of the full moon.

Say this prayer:

Holy Father, Lord of Hosts, Most High God, Font of Mercy, send forth your shimmering splendor through the gracious presence of your angel Gabriel. Send your good angel upon me that I may catch the light of the Moon and use it for all good purposes through this creature of water, which you have made sacred to and of the nature of the Moon. Let this mirror, which you have made by the light of the Moon catch its rays and reverberate them into the water that it might wholly be the shimmering light of the Moon's enchantment. St. Gabriel, gather for me Moonlight and hold it firm in this vessel that I might use it for all God's wonders.

Retrieve the Moon water the next morning and keep it in a safe dark place until the Moon begins to wax again.

When the waxing of the moon begins, each night that you are able, draw a bath. Place in the water some portion of your moon water, milk, honey, rose petals, damiana, and jasmine.

Pray this verse over the water:

And it came to pass in an eveningtide, that David arose from off his bed, and walked upon the roof of the king's house: and from the roof he saw a woman washing herself; and the woman was very beautiful to look upon.

Remove your clothes and say this prayer:

Holy Father, Lord of Hosts, Most High God, Font of Mercy, send forth your shimmering splendor through the gracious presence of your angel Gabriel. Send your good angel upon me that I may shine with the light of the Moon wrap me in splendor and the milky white starlight that I might enchant all who see me with wonder and beauty. Wrap me in glory that all will see me as beautiful.

Get in the water, soak and relax while praying these verses:

(11) Thy lips, O my spouse, drop as the honeycomb: honey and milk are under thy tongue; and the smell of thy garments is like the smell of Lebanon. (12) A garden inclosed is my sister, my spouse; a spring shut up, a fountain sealed. (13) Thy plants are an orchard of pomegranates, with pleasant fruits; camphire, with spikenard, (14) Spikenard and saffron; calamus and cinnamon, with all trees of frankincense; myrrh and aloes, with all the chief spices: (15) A fountain of gardens, a well of living waters, and streams from Lebanon. (16) Awake, O north wind; and come, thou south; blow upon my garden, that the spices thereof may flow out. Let my beloved come into his garden, and eat his pleasant fruits.

Repeat this as many nights as you are able until the full moon.

To Bring Rain

Paint the Sixth Pentacle of the Moon on a bowl and consecrate it using the ritual.

Fill the bowl with water – preferably rain water, spring water as a second option, thirdly any other water.

Draw this square:

S	A	G	R	I	R
A					
G					
R					
I					
R					

Touch the top of the square and say this prayer:

Holy Father, Lord of Hosts, Most High God, Font of Mercy, send forth your sonorous voice of thunder through the gracious presence of your angel Gabriel. Send your good angel upon me that I may receive at the heralding of his trumpet boundless rains. Gabriel bring forth cloud and thunder and open the skies as you did in the time of Noah. Water the fields, swell the rivers, pour forth the treasure of the firmament.

Place the square in the bowl saying:

All the fountains of the great deep were broken up…and the rain was upon the earth

Luminarium

Mars

To Separate Two People

Take a pair of red candles bound by a single wick. Carve the name of one of the people into one candle and the other into the other candle. Dress them with pepper oil rubbing counter clockwise away from you. If you wish one person to stay with you and the other to be sent away, rub clockwise and towards you for the person you wish to retain. Repeat their names as you carve them and as you dress the candles.

Set the candles as far apart as the wick will allow. Between them place the consecrated third pentacle of Mars. On top of the pentacle, place a sharpened knife or dagger. If you have items related to the individuals, place them by their respective candles.

Sprinkle everything with cayenne pepper.

Say this prayer:

Holy Father, Lord of Hosts, Most High God, Font of Mercy, send forth your might through the gracious presence of your angel Khamael. Send your good angel upon me that those who should be torn asunder are torn asunder as befitting of your mighty wrath. Khamael come forth and rend like a sword [Name] from [Name] such that they are cleaved apart irreparably and forever. Let all enmity grow between them so that they burn and suffer until they are apart.

Light the candles at the center of the joint wick so that it burns apart.

Pray the psalm

Psalm 127 *(1) Except the Lord build the house, they labour in vain that build it: except the Lord keep the city, the watchman waketh but in vain. (2) It is vain for you to rise up early, to sit up late, to eat the bread of sorrows: for so he giveth his beloved sleep. (3) Lo, children are an heritage of the Lord: and the fruit of the womb is his reward. (4) As arrows are in the hand of a mighty man; so are children of the youth. (5) Happy is the man that hath his quiver full of them: they shall not be ashamed, but they shall speak with the enemies in the gate.*

Walk away from it and let the candles burn down.

To Heal Someone from Afar

Take a consecrated paper second pentacle of Mars, a photo or item belonging to the sick person (if you have it), a red candle, and balsam oil, or balm of gilead, or some other healing oil. If there is an oil related to the particular afflicted body part, that may be used.

Set the items related to the person in your working space.

On the back of the pentacle, write the name of the sick person five times; rotate 90 degrees and write "good health" over the name five times. Around this write, while speaking, your intention for their recovery so that it makes an unbroken circle, without lifting your pen.

Dress the intention with a 5 spot of oil while saying the name of the sick person five times.

Dress the candle with oil while speaking your desire that the person be made well.

Place the paper with the pentacle face up and place the candle on it. As you light the candle say:

In Him was life, and the life was the light of man.

Holy Father, Lord of Hosts, Most High God, Font of Mercy, send forth your might through the gracious presence of your angel Khamael. Send your good angel upon me that the illness which afflicts [Name of the Sick Person] may be defeated. Bring them triumph that they may be healed from this illness. Let them rise victoriously in full health. Amen.

Knock five times, say

It is done!

Let the candle burn out, then place the talisman with the photo or item belonging to the sick person until they are well.

Mercury

To Open Roads

Consecrate the 5th pentacle of Mercury. Take an orange candle and carve your name into it. Dress it with road-opener oil from the middle to the top, and then the middle to the bottom.

Say this prayer:

Holy Father, Lord of Hosts, Most High God, Font of Mercy, send forth your righteous likeness through the gracious presence of your angel Michael. Send your good angel upon me that I may receive his aid in opening doors to the opportunities which you have graciously set before me. St. Michael by your whip and your sword turn back all spirits which would prevent my success or hold back my efforts, bring the keys of St. Peter to open all doors for me.

Light the candle and say this prayer and pray this psalm:

God before me
God behind me
I on Thy path, O God
Thou, O God, in my steps.
In the twistings of the road.
In the currents of the river.
Be with me by day.
Be with me by night.
Be with me by day and by night.

Psalm 24 *(1) The earth is the Lord's, and the fulness thereof; the world, and they that dwell therein. (2) For he hath founded it upon the seas, and established it upon the floods. (3) Who shall ascend into the hill of the Lord? or who shall stand in his holy place? (4) He that hath clean hands, and a pure heart; who hath not lifted up his soul unto vanity, nor sworn deceitfully. (5) He shall receive the blessing from the Lord, and righteousness from the God of his salvation. (6) This is the generation of them that seek him, that seek thy face, O Jacob. Selah. (7) Lift up your heads, O ye gates; and be ye lift up, ye everlasting doors; and the King of glory shall come in. (8) Who is this King of glory? The Lord strong and mighty, the Lord mighty in battle. (9) Lift up your heads, O ye gates; even lift them up, ye everlasting doors; and the King of glory shall come in. (10) Who is this King of glory? The Lord of hosts, he is the King of glory. Selah.*

Let the candle burn down, then place the remains of the candle and the pentacle in the nearest crossroads.

Luminarium

Jupiter

House Blessing

Write out the 61st Psalm on a piece of paper. On the other side, place the Seventh Pentacle of Jupiter. Consecrate them with the 113th Psalm.

Anoint the paper with a 5 spot of High John the Conqueror Oil and dress four blue candles with saffron oil. Place the candles on the corners of the paper.

Say this prayer:

Holy Father, Lord of Hosts, Most High God, Font of Mercy, send forth your fecundity and joy through the gracious presence of your angel Sachiel. Send your good angel upon me that my home and all those in it might receive his aid in acquiring securing luck, success, and prosperity as you have ordained for us. Sachiel in the name of the Lord of Hosts bring peace of mind by bringing good fortune and providence. Bless and protect this home from poverty and strife, let good fortune reside within these walls. Let this scroll be a barrier against misfortune.

Light the candles. Burn saffron incense. Pray the 61st Psalm over the candles and paper, then go from room to room praying the psalm with the saffron incense burning.

Psalm 61 *(1) Hear my cry, O God; attend unto my prayer. 2 From the end of the earth will I cry unto thee, when my heart is overwhelmed: lead me to the rock that is higher than I. 3 For thou hast been a shelter for me, and a strong tower from the enemy. 4 I will abide in thy tabernacle for ever: I will trust in the covert of thy wings. Selah. 5 For thou, O God, hast heard my vows: thou hast given me the heritage of those that fear thy name. 6 Thou wilt prolong the king's life: and his years as many generations. 7 He shall abide before God for ever: O prepare mercy and truth, which may preserve him. 8 So will I sing praise unto thy name for ever, that I may daily perform my vows.*

When the candles have burned down, roll the paper and wind it in blue ribbon. Hang it by your door.

Good Fortune Charm

To make a charm to bring luck wealth and good fortune to you, use this spell.

Consecrate a paper Second Pentacle of Jupiter. On the back of the paper, draw the kamea of Jupiter. Around the kamea, write your intention in an unbroken circle without lifting your pen, while speaking it out loud.

Anoint your intention with a 5 spot using High John the Conqueror Oil.

Fold the paper towards yourself three times.

Place the paper within a bit of blue fabric. Along with the paper, put in a silver coin, cedar chips, saffron threads, a High John the Conqueror Root, five-finger grass, and a magnet which has been dressed with iron filings. Anoint with High John oil. Spit into the bag and breathe on it focusing on stirring life within it. Fold the cloth over to hold everything and tie it shut.

Hold the bag close to your chest and say this prayer:

Holy Father, Lord of Hosts, Most High God, Font of Mercy, send forth your fecundity and joy through the gracious presence of your angel Sachiel. Send your good angel upon me that I may receive his aid in acquiring securing luck, success, and prosperity as you have ordained for me. Sachiel in the name of the Lord of Hosts bring peace of mind by bringing good fortune and providence. Bring life to this bag so that it may draw to me success, good fortune, and peace.

Hold the bag to your face and whisper the psalm to it:

Psalm 65 *(1) Praise waiteth for thee, O God, in Sion: and unto thee shall the vow be performed. (2) O thou that hearest prayer, unto thee shall all flesh come. (3) Iniquities prevail against me: as for our transgressions, thou shalt purge them away. (4) Blessed is the man whom thou choosest, and causest to approach unto thee, that he may dwell in thy courts: we shall be satisfied with the goodness of thy house, even of thy holy temple. (5) By terrible things in righteousness wilt thou answer us, O God of our salvation; who art the confidence of all the ends of the earth, and of them that are afar off upon the sea: (6) Which by his strength setteth fast the mountains; being girded with power: (7) Which stilleth the noise of the seas, the noise of their waves, and the tumult of the people. (8) They also that dwell in the uttermost parts are afraid at thy tokens: thou makest the outgoings of the morning and evening to rejoice. (9) Thou visitest the earth, and waterest it: thou greatly enrichest it with the river of God, which is full of water: thou preparest them corn, when thou hast so provided for it. (10) Thou waterest the ridges thereof abundantly: thou settlest the furrows thereof: thou makest it soft with showers: thou blessest the springing thereof. (11) Thou crownest the year with thy goodness; and thy paths drop fatness. (12) They drop upon the pastures of the wilderness: and the little hills rejoice on every side. (13) The pastures are clothed with flocks; the valleys also are covered over with corn; they shout for joy, they also sing.*

Carry the bag and sleep with it affixed to your chest. Anoint it each day. Do this for three days. After this the bag will live and will be able to work to draw people to you. Periodically anoint it and whisper the psalm to it to feed it.

Venus

To Obtain Many Friends and Lovers

To increase the number of friends and potential lovers around you, use this spell.

Consecrate the Third Pentacle of Venus on paper. On the back of the paper, draw the kamea of Venus. Around the kamea, write your intention in an unbroken circle without lifting your pen, while speaking it out loud.

Anoint your intention with a 5 spot, saying **IHVH, Adonai, Aegalmiel, Degaliel** with **Monachiel** in the center.

Fold the paper towards yourself three times.

Place the paper within a bit of red fabric. Along with the paper, put in rose petals, apple blossoms, honeysuckle, and a magnet which has been dressed with iron filings. Anoint with High John oil. Spit into the bag and breathe on it, focusing on stirring life within it. Fold the cloth over to hold everything and tie it shut.

Hold the bag close to your chest and say this prayer:

Holy Father, Lord of Hosts, Most High God, Font of Mercy, send forth your righteous love through the gracious presence of your angel Haniel. Send your good angel upon me that I may receive his aid in acquiring love and friendship. Haniel in the name of the Lord of Hosts bring new friends and lovers to me. Bring life to this bag so that it may draw together those who will love me.

Hold the bag to your face and whisper the psalm to it:

Psalm 33 *(1) Rejoice in the Lord, O ye righteous: for praise is comely for the upright. (2) Praise the Lord with harp: sing unto him with the psaltery and an instrument of ten strings. (3) Sing unto him a new song; play skilfully with a loud noise. (4) For the word of the Lord is right; and all his works are done in truth. (5) He loveth righteousness and judgment: the earth is full of the goodness of the Lord. (6) By the word of the Lord were the heavens made; and all the host of them by the breath of his mouth. (7) He gathereth the waters of the sea together as an heap: he layeth up the depth in storehouses. (8) Let all the earth fear the Lord: let all the inhabitants of the world stand in awe of him. (9) For he spake, and it was done; he commanded, and it stood fast. (10) The Lord bringeth the counsel of the heathen to nought: he maketh the devices of the people of none effect. (11) The counsel of the Lord standeth for ever, the thoughts of his heart to all generations. (12) Blessed is the nation whose God is the Lord; and the people whom he hath chosen for his own inheritance. (13) The Lord looketh from heaven; he beholdeth all the sons of men. (14) From the place of his habitation he looketh upon all the inhabitants of the earth. (15) He fashioneth their hearts alike; he considereth all their works. (16) There is no king saved by the multitude of an host: a mighty man is not delivered by much strength. (17) An horse is a vain thing for safety: neither shall he deliver any by his great strength. (18) Behold, the eye of the Lord is upon them that fear him, upon them that hope in his mercy; (19) To deliver their soul from death, and to keep them alive in famine. (20) Our soul waiteth for the Lord: he is our help and our shield. (21) For our heart shall rejoice in him, because we have trusted in his holy name. (22) Let thy mercy, O Lord, be upon us, according as we hope in thee.*

Carry the bag and sleep with it affixed to your chest. Anoint it each day. Do this for three days. After this, the bag will live and be able to work to draw people to you. Periodically anoint it and whisper the psalm to it to feed it.

To Obtain a Particular Lover

Should you desire the love of a particular person, use this spell. If you have a picture of the object of your affection, or an item belonging to them, or a sample of their handwriting, place this with the seal as you perform the spell.

Consecrate a paper Fifth Pentacle of Venus.

Carve the name of the person you desire into a red candle and dress it with rose oil or Come-to-Me oil, rotating clockwise and towards you. Repeat the name of the person you want seven times while dressing it.

Say this prayer while holding the candle

Holy Father, Lord of Hosts, Most High God, Font of Mercy, send forth your righteous love through the gracious presence of your angel Haniel. Send your good angel upon me that I may receive his aid in acquiring the love of [Name]. Haniel in the name of the Lord of Hosts bring [Name] to me and let love flower between us.

Place the candle on the seal and light the candle saying:

My heart is like wax, it is melted in the midst of my bowels.

Let the candle burn down. You can carry the seal and wax as a talisman and wear the oil when you will see the person you desire.

Luminarium

Saturn

Wash Away Enemy

Should you have an enemy you wish to vex and send away.

Consecrate the Fourth Pentacle of Saturn on rice paper. Obtain a bottle of sparkling wine and mustard.

Say this prayer while holding the pentacle:

Holy Father, Lord of Hosts, Most High God, Font of Mercy, send forth your finality through the grave presence of your angel Cassiel. Send your good angel upon me that I may have aid against the unrighteous and the vexations of those who turn from goodness. Great angel Cassiel come to my aid against the sins of [Name] who has been set against me. Utterly destroy [Name] that I might receive God's protection from the unrighteous.

Place the pentacle into the bottle of wine so that it will dissolve therein. Pour in some of the mustard and reseal the wine.

For three nights, pray this psalm over the bottle

(1) Hold not thy peace, O God of my praise; (2) For the mouth of the wicked and the mouth of the deceitful are opened against me: they have spoken against me with a lying tongue. (3) They compassed me about also with words of hatred; and fought against me without a cause. (4) For my love they are my adversaries: but I give myself unto prayer. (5) And they have rewarded me evil for good, and hatred for my love. (6) Set thou a wicked man over him: and let Satan stand at his right hand. (7) When he shall be judged, let him be condemned: and let his prayer become sin. (8) Let his days be few; and let another take his office. (9) Let his children be fatherless, and his wife a widow. (10) Let his children be

continually vagabonds, and beg: let them seek their bread also out of their desolate places. (11) Let the extortioner catch all that he hath; and let the strangers spoil his labour. (12) Let there be none to extend mercy unto him: neither let there be any to favour his fatherless children. (13) Let his posterity be cut off; and in the generation following let their name be blotted out. (14) Let the iniquity of his fathers be remembered with the Lord; and let not the sin of his mother be blotted out. (15) Let them be before the Lord continually, that he may cut off the memory of them from the earth. (16) Because that he remembered not to shew mercy, but persecuted the poor and needy man, that he might even slay the broken in heart. (17) As he loved cursing, so let it come unto him: as he delighted not in blessing, so let it be far from him. (18) As he clothed himself with cursing like as with his garment, so let it come into his bowels like water, and like oil into his bones. (19) Let it be unto him as the garment which covereth him, and for a girdle wherewith he is girded continually. (20) Let this be the reward of mine adversaries from the Lord, and of them that speak evil against my soul. (21) But do thou for me, O God the Lord, for thy name's sake: because thy mercy is good, deliver thou me. (22) For I am poor and needy, and my heart is wounded within me. (23) I am gone like the shadow when it declineth: I am tossed up and down as the locust. (24) My knees are weak through fasting; and my flesh faileth of fatness. (25) I became also a reproach unto them: when they looked upon me they shaked their heads. (26) Help me, O Lord my God: O save me according to thy mercy: (27) That they may know that this is thy hand; that thou, Lord, hast done it. (28) Let them curse, but bless thou: when they arise, let them be ashamed; but let thy servant rejoice. (29) Let mine adversaries be clothed with shame, and let them cover themselves with their own confusion, as with a mantle. (30) I will greatly praise the Lord with my mouth; yea, I will praise him among the multitude. (31) For he shall stand at the right hand of the poor, to save him from those that condemn his soul.

After the third night, pour the mixture upon the steps of your enemy's home, but make sure that none of it touches you. As you pour it out say:

As he clothed himself with cursing like as with a garment, so let it come unto his bowels like water, and like oil into his bones.

To Destroy a Building

On one side of a piece of paper, draw the Seventh Pentacle of Saturn. On the other side draw the square appropriate to your goal:

N	A	V	E	H
A		Q		.
V	Q			.
E				
H				D

To make a House fall to the ground

Q	A	Q	A	H
A				
Q				Q
A				
H			Q	Q

To destroy a Town

Luminarium

O	O	M	A	H	O	N
O					
M			Q		
A		Q			
H					
O					
N					

To demolish Strongholds

Around the square write your goal regarding what needs to be destroyed. As with the other spells write it in an unbroken circle and do not lift your pen.

If you can obtain a map which shows the location you wish to be impacted, place that upon the altar. You will also need a black candle and a metal bowl.

This should be performed within the full conjuration.

Call upon the Gnomes in the ritual.

Call upon Cassiel and the Aerial Spirits; request that Cassiel call forth the orders of angels and Astaroth to aid in performing the work at hand.

Say this prayer:

By Cassiel and in the name of the Lord of Hosts I call upon The Hayyoth, by Cassiel and in the name of the Lord of Hosts I call upon the Ophanim, by Cassiel and in the name of the Lord of Hosts I call upon the Aralim, by Cassiel and in the name of the Lord of Hosts I call upon the Chashmalim, by Cassiel and in the name of the Lord of Hosts I call upon the Seraphim, by Cassiel and in the name of the Lord of Hosts I call upon the Malakim, by Cassiel and in the name of the Lord of Hosts I call upon the Elohim, by Cassiel and in the name of the Lord of Hosts I call upon the Beni Elohim, by Cassiel and in the name of the Lord of Hosts I call upon the Kerubim by call the orders of angels I call upon the might to shake the foundations of the Earth and set the world to tremble. By all the angels of heaven I call upon and bind Astaroth to bring about this destruction

Request that Cassiel consecrate the pentacle, and that he command the aerial spirits and Astaroth to carry out the work.

Place the seal on the map and strike the map with your fist three times. Then light the candle and burn the seal. As you light the seal say:

As this is destroyed so shall be [the place].

Pray the psalm while the seal burns in the bowl.

Psalm 18 *(1) I will love thee, O Lord, my strength. (2) The Lord is my rock, and my fortress, and my deliverer; my God, my strength, in whom I will trust; my buckler, and the horn of my salvation, and my high tower. (3) I will call upon the Lord, who is worthy to be praised: so shall I be saved from mine enemies. (4) The sorrows of death compassed me, and the floods of ungodly men made me afraid. (5) The sorrows of hell compassed me about: the snares of death prevented me. (6) In my distress I called upon the Lord, and cried unto my God: he heard my voice out of his temple, and my cry came before him, even into his ears. (7) Then the earth shook and trembled; the foundations also of the hills moved and were shaken, because he was wroth. (8) There went up a smoke out of his nostrils, and fire out of his mouth devoured: coals were kindled by it. (9) He bowed the heavens also, and came down: and darkness was under his feet. (10) And he rode upon a cherub, and did fly: yea, he did fly upon the wings of the wind. (11) He made darkness his secret place;*

his pavilion round about him were dark waters and thick clouds of the skies. (12) At the brightness that was before him his thick clouds passed, hail stones and coals of fire. (13) The Lord also thundered in the heavens, and the Highest gave his voice; hail stones and coals of fire. (14) Yea, he sent out his arrows, and scattered them; and he shot out lightnings, and discomfited them. (15) Then the channels of waters were seen, and the foundations of the world were discovered at thy rebuke, O Lord, at the blast of the breath of thy nostrils. (16) He sent from above, he took me, he drew me out of many waters. (17) He delivered me from my strong enemy, and from them which hated me: for they were too strong for me. (18) They prevented me in the day of my calamity: but the Lord was my stay. (19) He brought me forth also into a large place; he delivered me, because he delighted in me. (20) The Lord rewarded me according to my righteousness; according to the cleanness of my hands hath he recompensed me. (21) For I have kept the ways of the Lord, and have not wickedly departed from my God. (22) For all his judgments were before me, and I did not put away his statutes from me. (23) I was also upright before him, and I kept myself from mine iniquity. (24) Therefore hath the Lord recompensed me according to my righteousness, according to the cleanness of my hands in his eyesight. (25) With the merciful thou wilt shew thyself merciful; with an upright man thou wilt shew thyself upright; (26) With the pure thou wilt shew thyself pure; and with the froward thou wilt shew thyself froward. (27) For thou wilt save the afflicted people; but wilt bring down high looks. (28) For thou wilt light my candle: the Lord my God will enlighten my darkness. (29) For by thee I have run through a troop; and by my God have I leaped over a wall. (30) As for God, his way is perfect: the word of the Lord is tried: he is a buckler to all those that trust in him. (31) For who is God save the Lord? or who is a rock save our God? (32) It is God that girdeth me with strength, and maketh my way perfect. (33) He maketh my feet like hinds' feet, and setteth me upon my high places. (34) He teacheth my hands to war, so that a bow of steel is broken by mine arms. (35) Thou hast also given me the shield of thy salvation: and thy right hand hath holden me up, and thy gentleness hath made me great. (36) Thou hast enlarged my steps under me, that my feet did not slip. (37) I have pursued mine enemies, and overtaken them: neither did I turn again till they were consumed. (38) I have wounded them that they were not able to rise: they are fallen under my feet. (39) For thou hast girded me with strength unto the battle: thou hast subdued under me those that rose up against me. (40) Thou hast also given me the necks of mine enemies; that I might destroy them that hate me. (41) They cried, but there was none to save them: even unto the Lord, but he answered them not. (42) Then did I beat them small as the dust before the wind: I did cast them out as the dirt in the streets. (43) Thou hast delivered me from the strivings of the people; and thou hast made me the head of the heathen: a people whom I have not known shall serve me. (44) As soon as they hear of me, they shall obey me: the strangers shall submit themselves unto me. (45) The strangers shall fade away, and be afraid out of their close places. (46) The Lord liveth; and blessed be my rock; and let the God of my salvation be exalted. (47) It is God that avengeth me, and subdueth the people under me. (48) He delivereth me from mine enemies: yea, thou liftest me up above those that rise up against me: thou hast delivered me from the violent man. (49) Therefore will I give thanks unto thee, O Lord, among the heathen, and sing praises unto thy name. (50) Great deliverance giveth he to his king; and sheweth mercy to his anointed, to David, and to his seed for evermore.

When the seal has burned to ash, offer the spirits what payment you will give them and license them to depart to do their work.

Take the ash out to the crossroads; pour it on the ground describing the place you intend to be destroyed. Stomp on the ash three times saying:

Then the earth shook and trembled, the foundations of the hills also moved and were shaken, because He was wroth

Recipes and Materials

One of the purposes of this text is to provide a system of magic that someone can pick up and run with, even if they don't have a lot of experience or access to materials. Various situations can cause limitations on what materials we have access to. You could strip this system down to purely things you can find in your home, candles, a bowl of water, a pebble, a bit of grape vine, a coin, and some red cloth. You can get by without much of the other things. Be clever. Figure out options for the stuff you need, figure out options for adapting.

Don't strip everything out to make it easy, but don't let a missing piece stop you from trying the work. The system is somewhat modular and adaptable. The tools can, in most cases, be substituted for something similar. The bowl could be replaced by a wine glass, or a jar; the lamp could be replaced by a candle. Real incense is better than cones or sticks, but if cones or sticks are what you have, try it with that.

As far as materials, the ones more likely to not be in people's random household possessions are the oils. You can replace any of the oils referenced with an oil that does something similar. If there is an herb or spice you have access to which has powers similar to a referenced oil, you can use that herb to make an oil.

To help make things easier, I'm presenting recipes for some of the referenced oils. Psalms appropriate to their work, or blues songs about them, can be recited over them when you make them. The same process for waking up herbs and incenses should be used for the ingredients. Setting the container of oil on a consecrated pentacle, or consecrating the oil in a conjuration ritual are options as well for empowering them.

The simplest way to approach these if you're just anointing candles or papers is to macerate the ingredients in a carrier oil. Grinding the ingredients with a bit of carrier oil can help open them so their essence can be absorbed. Some recipes or ingredients can be macerated in alcohol and then a few drops of the resulting tincture can be added to a carrier oil.

This is not at all intended as thorough instruction in oil making or a thorough collection of recipes. This is, very much so, a quick and dirty approach. This is just to give you an option if you don't have access to materials.

Some of the oils listed can be made with a single ingredient. High John the Conqueror, Pepper Oil, Balm of Gilead Oil, Saffron Oil, Hyssop Oil, and Balsam Oil can all be made with just the carrier oil and the ingredient for which it is named. For High John the Conqueror you'll need a High John the Conqueror Root, a piece of the root should remain in the oil once it's prepared. For pepper oil use cayenne pepper. For balm of gilead use balm buds, a bud from poplar trees. A small amount of saffron threads will work for the saffron oil. For hyssop oil use hyssop. Balsam fur, balsam poplar, or peru balsam can be used for making balsam oil.

Light or extra light olive oil – not extra virgin olive oil; is a readily available oil which can be used as a carrier oil. Sweet almond is a popular carrier oil which has benefits for skin and hair and preservative properties. Grapeseed and jojoba oil are popular options as well.

Here are some recipe options for the named oils. There are many other recipes out there as well.

Crown of Success Oil

3 bay leaves
3 whole cloves
1 cinnamon stick broken into 3 pieces
Dried orange peel
Woodruff
Frankincense resin crushed to powder or frankincense essential oil
Sandalwood crushed to powder or sandalwood essential oil
Vetiver roots or resin crushed to powder or vetiver essential oil

Gold leaf flakes or dust or scrap gold or pyrite chunk

Abramelin Oil

Galangal
Myrrh
Cinnamon

King Solomon Wisdom Oil

Hyssop
Solomon Seal
Bay leaf
Frankincense
Rose

Send Back Evil Oil

Lemon Grass
Hyssop
Angelica
Verbena
Peppermint
Calendula
Devil's Shoe Strings
A Piece of Smoky Quartz

Road Opener Oil

Orange Peel
Lemon Peel
Sandalwood
Abre Camino
Five Finger Grass

Uncrossing Oil

Lavender
Rose
Lemon Juice
Bay Leaves
Verbena
A Pinch of Bergamot

Come To Me Oil

Bee Pollen
Red Pepper Flakes
Licorice Roots
Rose Petals
Vanilla
A Piece of Rose Quartz
A Lodestone fed with iron filings

    If you can't acquire or make an oil don't let that stop you. If you have some olive oil you can consecrate that through prayer. If you need it consecrated for a particular purpose, write the power to which you want it consecrated on rice paper, dissolve the rice paper into the oil and pray invoking those powers to consecrate the oil. This should be your last possible solution.

Experiences

Once a usable draft of this book was complete, I organized a group of people to read and experiment with it. The idea behind the book was to present a system of magic that allowed magicians to fast track their preparation and amp up the experience. It was also supposed to be simple enough that people could do it with limited access to stores and equipment. I wanted perspectives on how it worked and how it was presented. This experimental group tested out the preparations and the rituals for a few weeks and shared their experiences. They also gave some feedback on how the information is presented and helped edit the text. It was very useful.

Feedback, insights, and edits came from about six people. I have experiences to present from four of them. The group in general had broadly ranging experience levels with magic. One of the people who received a draft text had no experience of magic at all, another had completed the Abramelin working. The full breath of experience levels between these was represented, with a focus on inviting magicians closer to the beginner through intermediate range.

To present their experiences I have reworked the explanations they shared with me. What is presented here are not exactly their first-person accounts, but are assembled from their accounts with some editing, and commentary.

Tester One: Aequus

Podcaster and blogger Aequus Nox was one of the experimenters who helped test the system. She has been exploring magic for about a year and was one of the people approaching the system with the freshest eyes. When I asked her, I figured she would be a good candidate for testing it out with a perspective not so far removed from anyone picking up the book and just starting out.

She found that gathering the items was not particularly difficult. Many of them were things she had on hand already. Hopefully this will be the experience for most people. In Aequus's case she has been exploring magic for about a year, so that may have made some things more readily handy. Most items can probably be picked up between a visit to the grocery store, the Wal-Mart and maybe Target or a craft store. Otherwise they should be accessible through Amazon if you're in a situation where occult stores are unavailable.

She tried the ritual without the wand. She used a candle in lieu of the lamp. She was able to obtain grape wood from her mother in law. A bit of grape vine from a bundle of grapes works well for this. Searching through an old change jar she was able to fine a silver bearing coin. While we can work with any silver colored coin the silver metal is additive. Searching through old accumulated coins, or picking up a few rolls of coins from the bank might result in an old coin that bears silver. A quick Google search will tell you what years to look for. She was able to get a magnet from her husband, who harvested it from his miniatures. She was able to find a pebble outside and mark it with the necessary number with a Sharpie. She wore regular clothes for her ritual attire. From exploring magic, she already had an incense burner, frankincense and myrrh, charcoal, offering bowls and Abramelin oil. She had white tea lights to use for candles, which most households should have on hand. She had wine, which again, is common to have around, and the red cloth. Her collection of tools illustrates clearly how easy putting the tools for this together is. Most of it is not anything special or difficult to attain.

    Aequus started with setting up the altar space the night before the conjuration. She cleaned everything up then welcomed her ancestors. The next day, the day of Mercury, she began a few hours before planning to do the conjuration. She cleaned the altar with Florida Water and then Holy Water. Then she blessed the candles and woke up the incense. She finished up the set-up of the space by doing the ancestor service. Aequus and I have discussed ancestor work in the past. It's something she's wanted to do but has struggled to work with. She felt her attempts here were successful. She clearly felt the presence of her ancestors. She said that she could feel the presence of spirits but they felt familiar. She said the feeling that they were with her was hugely different from other attempts. She was able to chat with them, and finished up happy and giggling, inviting them to stay. She has since continued to maintain the altar and the relationship.

    After calling upon her ancestors she took a ritual bath with Abramelin oil. She used herbs and water to make the khernips, and did that using cleansing prayers before heading to the altar. She did pranayama and the Headless Invocation along with a prayer to her angel. She worked on Wednesday and called upon Michael. She chose not to attempt calling the aerial king for now. When she got through the conjurations, she felt the temperature perceptibly drop in the room. She felt goosebumps on her skin. She did not see Michael, but saw movement from the south. She could feel the presence of someone in the room with her. When she finished the conjuration there was a strong burst of scent from the incense. There was a distinct flicker to the candle light during the spirit's presence.

    Aequus asked Michael for help with a promotion for her husband. In order for him to get the promotion he needed to complete some IT classes. He was enrolled but waiting for money to be right. After the conjuration he received an email offering him $300 to take the classes. He impressed his manager, and he received a surprise $100 bonus gift card from his employer. So, two things occurred to move him closer to the promotion, and he is netting $400 in bonus money for taking steps towards the promotion. None of these monies not the opportunity to impress the boss were expected prior to working magic.

Tester Two: Jonathan

    Jonathan Masters has been involved in the OTO and ceremonial magic for several years. Over the last few years, he has been developing a personal practice of conjuration. He is, in my summation, a good example of how an intermediate practitioner would approach the material in this book.

    He had explored possibly beginning the Abramelin working a few years ago and decided to hold off. Prior to my inviting him to be part of the test team for this book, he had prayed to Hekate for ways to be open for him to pursue his Angel. After reading the draft he expressed that the prayers and methods given in this book were what he was looking for in that regard.

    Prior to starting Jonathan asked about me about substitutions regarding the ancestor service and the oil lamp. He ended up using an oil lamp and the ancestor service method described in the text. Answering this is a good opportunity though to bring up the idea of substitutions. The oil lamp is useful because the oil can be consecrated and augmented with oils and herbs. The adjustable wick allows for a perceptible action in which you can manipulate the light, which physically represents your angel, as you call upon your angel. The lamp also has a particular association with the magician, or the guiding light. None of these elements is really necessary. A lantern using a candle, or just a candle by itself, is sufficient. A small torch, a brazier, or a fire bowl could work too. As for the ancestor service, if there is a practice you have that works use that. Think of this as a modular piece. If you want something different than what we've presented it just needs to fit into that space in the same way. It needs to accomplish the same things. If it's just a matter of different religious iconography, use the religious modality that suits you, but maintain the same structure.

    The week before engaging in the actual conjuration Jonathan took a meal with his ancestors and began to set up the altar as described in the book. He also began a daily regimen of prayers and activities based on instructions from the text. After this set-up he described doing the ancestor service. He had a conversation with them, stated his intentions, and offered nuts and water. He said he could see a visible aura around the offerings as they were accepted. The tea lights he used burned for about five hours rather than the one hour he expected. I have had this experience in the past using this approach to working with ancestors. In one example, it was my maternal grandfather's birthday, I was asking him to help my mother. Instead of the eight hours or so over which my votive candles usually burned his stayed lit for most of a week. This kind of persistence of presence is not an unusual physical sign.

 A few days after the ancestor working, Jonathan conjured Gabriel. He prepared the space and tools using Angel Water as he did not have access to Holy Water. He followed the ritual script as presented in the text. He said there was a rather noticeable increase in wind blowing through the windows when he called upon Hekate. He found the Invocation of the Lamp to be a potent addition to the process. The Invocation of the Lamp created a sense of euphoria for him. He found that he was very "in the zone" when reciting the barbarous names and they were easy to recite without rehearsal. He asked Gabriel to appear visibly and saw an image form through the interaction of the oil, the grape-wood and the water. He said the nature of the initial vision was along the lines of "troubling the waters," and took on a Lovecraftian like image of swirling eyes. The visual broke down a bit, and continued in the form of smoke or steam rising from the water, and the bowl seemed to grow. When he told Gabriel that he wanted to make a request he heard "ask" as if a dozen voices were speaking in his head at once. The sensation was unpleasant and left him with a headache. He had missed using the red cloth; he was swept up in the rest of the ritual. This may have caused some of the inconsistency in the visionary experience.

Luminarium

Jonathan requested that his dreams be empowered with greater lucidity and easier recall. He has had vivid dreams nightly since.

As a follow up experiment, Jonathan tried slightly modifying the method to conjure a demon. When he presented this idea, I explained that the method presented in this text was originally used for conjuring a demon in a group ritual. There are some variations in the opening pieces, but the structure, the Invocation of the Lamp, and other portions are more or less the same. The demonic version has a few additional parts after conjuring the angel. The initial use of the ritual involved a separate scryer. She said that she had an easier time scrying, and a more vivid experience than she had in previous conjurations, using the method presented here. In that ritual individuals made pacts with the demon one on one. Each person wrote their request and what offering they would make. They burned the request to communicate it to the spirit, and the scryer confirmed with the spirit whether or not it was accepted. I have heard about several results that were achieved using this method including someone obtaining around $30K. Another person got a difficult coworker removed despite the coworker being the boss's best friend. Another person obtained a piece of property they were trying to get despite several difficulties that were in the way.

Jonathan attempted his demonic conjuration without knowledge of the original form of the ritual. He dropped some of the initial pieces from the ritual. He began with the ancestor service. He called upon a demon with whom he had worked previously. He conjured extemporaneously. The demon arrived giving the appearance of gray steam arising from the bowl. The vision became clearer, Jonathan described it as "super creepy, faint little twitchy stuff" that occurred with the arrival. He wore the red cloth this time. He said it helped immensely in comparison with the previous attempt to see the spirit. He also added a phylactery for protection, and a triangle around the scrying bowl to localize the spirit's presence. His feeling after working with this method was that it can definitely be approached modularly so long as the lamp and the ancestor altar are used effectively.

Luminarium

Tester Three: Anneliese

Anneliese Anthoinette is one of our newer magicians, although you wouldn't know it to talk with her – she carries herself with gravitas, and confidence that suggests experience. She is one of the people who seems able to help connect and organize people in the magical community, with ease. She has been practicing magic for about two years without the aid of groups or orders, but in her own words she has "studied under a variety of amazing teachers." She did her first conjuration about a year ago. Recently she approached me about an experiment she and some friends were looking to do. This effort to experiment and her general helpfulness and supportiveness made me realize she would be a great person to include in this.

Anneliese's approach to the practical end of preparing might be useful for people. Magic can often get swept aside because preparation is inconvenient. You have to get your ritual script, get your materials, set aside time, and set up and prepare the space. I have written before about the utility of having your regularly used rituals written out or preprinted so you can just pull them out on the fly. This book is actually designed intentionally to serve that purpose. One of our other testers noted in his feedback that he copied the rituals into his personal magic book. Along these lines, keeping tools pre-prepared and stored so you can just open a drawer and grab and go is another way to make it easier. Being comfortable in the space and with the ritual will also make it feel less uncomfortable.

To the end of being comfortable and ready, Anneliese's notes reflect a very studious approach. She wrote questions in her margins then reread the text to see if the answers were there. She kept a separate set of notes to write down everything the text had related to the spirit she intended to conjure. She took notes on all the things she would need and steps she would perform. She wanted a fuller lay of the land so she set up her ritual space and did a dry run of the purifications, the consecrations, and the ritual itself, adding to her notes as she did the run through. This is actually the approach I take when setting up large group rituals. It's the best way to make sure you have all your materials and they're set in a convenient place. Anneliese's walk through revealed to her that she needed more candles.

 Anneliese took an interesting approach to the scrying bowl. She wanted the barbarous names visible on the bowl but did not want to create a permanent bowl yet for this system. So, she took a shallow glass dish and placed the names – written on a piece of paper; underneath the dish. She likewise used a paper pentacle she had made, but also had a professionally made and consecrated Jovial pentacle present.

 Like our other testers, Anneliese had some fun synchronicities involved in preparing to begin and gathering tools. People have often noted that the committed intention to do magic seems to set something in motion around that magic. Spirits are there, they want to be contacted – not necessarily all spirits, but many of the ones with whom we will work. She already had a candle consecrated to her Guardian Angel, as well as a consecrated ring, consecrated Jupiter oil, and as we mentioned – a Jupiter pentacle. These were all obtained from various professional magicians. She had consecrated olive oil, Abramelin oil, frankincense, and Holy Water on hand.

 The items of interesting circumstance in her preparation were the grape-wood, the wine, and the magnet. She had not realized she had a grape vine growing in her yard, and was able to use this to gather the needed material. She normally does not have wine at home, but her husband received a free bottle of wine as she was making her preparations and gathering her tools. The cork was marked with a crossroads symbol and the wine was named for the angels – Angela. She did not have a magnet until one arrived randomly in the mail, unrequested, the day of the conjuration.

 Anneliese had a permanently set up ancestor altar already. She regularly does work with her ancestors. So, she began that part of the process first, prior to the ritual bath. This restructures a little, but it does so in a way which more completely encompasses your pre-ritual components within the magical space of the ritual itself. She washed while praying the psalm, and then ritually cleansed herself with water and Abramelin oil. She used bottled spring water with wild sage and hyssop from her garden for the khernips. She donned her robe and went to the altar to begin.

    She followed the script for the ritual but with some interesting variations. While doing the initial parts prior to the invocations she continually utilized hesychastic prayer. I think this is a great approach, building spiritual fire as part of the background state of the ritual. I have utilized this type of practice while celebrating Mass. She, like Aequus, found the khernips a bit unfamiliar, and admittedly, it is not common to modern ceremonial magic. Based on her notes it sounds like she executed it smoothly, simply bringing the herbs to the point of smoldering and dropping them into the water. When she got to the invocations, she added another variation. She recited each invocation three times rather than one. This is great, repetition can help create needed spiritual states. Anneliese was moved to repetition by the enjoyment of the beauty of the hymns. She figured if it was pleasing to her it would be pleasing to the spirits being called. This is an astute and, in my view, correct analysis. This also illustrates how sometimes in rituals you will be inspired to make changes on-the-fly. Learn to quickly recognize and interpret this inspiration so you can decide when to follow it; sometimes it will provide really useful approaches and insights.

    While calling upon Hekate, Anneliese recognized a scent she associates with Hekate, and knew that indicated Hekate's presence. She says the scent came in strong. This is a good illustration of the fact that occult senses aren't only about sight, but are about all of our senses. Spirits can communicate their presence in many ways. When she got to the conjuration of Sachiel, she didn't notice anything happening until the final line of the conjuration. She did not get a visual but rather had a deep and moving sense of presence. I like her description so I'm going to quote her here:

"However, I did feel the same deeply all-encompassing compassionate feeling I had gotten when I did the Arbatel ritual for Bethor. I felt enveloped, or wrapped in a warm **VASTNESS**.

I felt "**SEEN**" in all my smallness but also in all my "too muchness". But I wasn't "too much" in that moment because there was **SO MUCH VASTNESS** it was enough to make even my too-muchness become inconsequential in comparison. It wasn't a feeling of Love, but more a feeling of deep, immeasurable, and truly **ABIDING** acceptance. Observed, seen, accepted. Because there is more than enough room.

A slightly numb observer part of me felt that crying would be appropriate, but there was such a vastness of calm, that there were no tears."

Both angels and demons often convey huge natures that impact human experience in ways beyond sight and sound. Personally, I think these experiences can give us a greater understanding and connection than seeing a goblin in a bowl. Sachiel is one of the loftier angels, inhabiting one of the highest heavens. I always find it interesting that people call upon him for such personal human matters, when to me he is so immense and transpersonal in his nature. Anneliese called with no desire but connection and interaction, and so she got to experience that depth and immensity.

    After talking with Sachiel she performed the license to depart, clocking about seventy minutes for the whole process, which is roughly within the range of the length of daytime planetary hours during the time of year in which the conjuration was done.

<u>Luminarium</u>

Tester Four: Alexander

    Our fourth tester was Alexander Deckman. Alexander traveled around Asia after high school and spent time living at a Shingon Buddhist Temple in Japan. Later, he worked on a rural tea farm in the mountains of Taiwan. While there, part of his duties involved service to the local spirits. After leaving Asia, traditional tea ceremonies and random adventures with spirits shaped his spiritual work. Eventually he found the OTO, which led to developing a more formal magical and spiritual practice. His practice wasn't Thelemic, or in line with modern ceremonial magic, but rather devotional work with Hermes. He grew this with work with the Greek Magical Papyri, and eventually work with a living statue hosting a Mercurial daimon. He is another example of an intermediate practitioner exploring the system, but one with a very low key and naturalistic approach to his work with spirits.

    It only took Alexander a couple of days to put together all the tools and materials. This kicked off an immersion in magic for him. He had been petitioning his spirits to bring new teaching and new opportunities to him. Within weeks of these petitions, I invited him to the *Luminarium* Beta Tester Team. After he finished reading *Luminarium* he accepted an invitation to a magical ritual of the Saints that I was organizing. So, he had his tool gathering, his normal devotional work, preparing to work with Saints and dead witches, and preparing for his *Luminarium* conjurations – and using the preparatory techniques which go with that. He felt that this was the literal answer to his petitions and prayers.

    About a year ago, I believe for his birthday, I had given Alexander a brass PELE ring I had made. He had been planning to consecrate it since then and decided to use his *Luminarium* experimentation for that purpose. He felt Michael would be appropriate for consecrating the ring as it is Michael who gives Dee the ring in Dee's scrying sessions.

    When he completed the conjuration to consecrate the ring, he felt that the experience had unlocked a whole new level for him. He felt that this approach helped him understand what he was doing and connect all the pieces in what he had been doing. He expressed that it allowed him to access angelic magic in a way he hadn't been able to before. He felt that he had access to more conviction, purpose and intention through this approach.

    Alexander wrote up a very thorough accounting of his experience, so I've edited it a bit and will present it as he stated it.

    "The ritual went very well. This was definitely my most involved ritual project to date as I still have a ritual to do tomorrow as well, that also coincides with the full moon. For this first operation I was fasting and abstaining from alcohol and other pleasurable indulgences for 24 hours prior to the work. Each day (the day before, as well as today) consisted of extensive prayers and purifications. All prayers were either directly pulled from *Luminarium* or were directly from the heart. Each night I was up all night until morning preparing, praying, and transcribing the entire working ritual – prayers and all; into my own personal book of magic.

    Each day at sunrise I prayed extensively before my altar and lamp before reciting the Orphic Hymn of the day and going to bed and sleeping until the afternoon. Today I felt as if I was floating for the entire day. I was in a solemn but very joyful state of mind all day. I broke the day into three pieces by which to work the ritual. In the second hour of Mercury I performed my usual Headless Rite along with weekly devotional ritual to Hermes and to my personal daimon. I told them of the work to come and asked them to aid me in it. After this I went to meditate, have a tea ceremony, and pray. The next part was the cleansing and preparation of the ritual space and took place during the 3rd Hour of Mercury. While cleansing the space, in the manner suggested in *Luminarium*, I prayed constant Hail Mary's while scrubbing the carpet, cleaning the furniture, and wiping everything with Holy Water.

Luminarium

I made a large amount of hyssop water which I added to the Holy Water and the cleaning solutions.

Once the cleaning was done, I performed my Ancestor service, calling upon St. Peter to open the gates of Heaven and Hell, Hermanubis to guide my blessed dead out of the land of Shadow, and Mary Queen of Heaven and Hell to bring forth my beloved dead. I finished my ancestral service as described in *Luminarium* and finalized the blessing of the space. I left the space had a second and more serious tea ceremony, reflecting, praying, and preparing for the final ritual. At this point the energy I was feeling was very intense and I had to stop and center myself on multiple occasions. Very fluttery, powerful waves would occasionally overtake me. They were in a way both very comfortable and yet also overwhelming.

Thirty minutes before the 4th hour of Mercury. Everything was set and prepared and I entered the bathroom to begin the pre-ritual. I prayed Psalm 27 aloud before entering the shower. I bathed and washed myself all the while repeating the versicle. While washing I envisioned my sins and impurities being washed away in divine light. I turned the water off and then doused my head in hyssop water and anointed my head with hyssop oil while praying Psalm 51. Then I dried myself with a fresh towel and walked into the next room nude. I preformed the first khernips washed myself of miasma and donned the ritual robes reciting the appropriate psalm. Then I made my way up the candlelit steps to the loft where the ritual was to take place.

At the top of the steps I called upon my Angel and said a Hail Mary. I entered the space and began the ritual. Everything went according to plan. Nothing went wrong. Everything flowed well and felt comfortable. There was, however, a point of doubt that entered my mind. I wondered that I might not be able to conjure the angel, but it was a fleeting thought easily and smoothly assuaged with the reassurance that even in failure there is success and that this experience itself, even up to this point, has taught me enough to consider the ritual as a glaring success whether the angel comes or not.

I followed the ritual entirely as it was written. It felt as if everything was working properly, and as I reached the Invocation of the Lamp things were definitely turned up a notch. It was fiery, for lack of a better term, and the flame danced beautifully in tandem with my words as I spoke them. After the invocation, I took a moment to be quiet and center myself. Mentally set myself to the task at hand, and the conjuration to come.

I recited the hymn of Mercury by heart as I have done hundreds of times before, then paused. I said a prayer to my angel, one to Hermes, and then to God – asking for their aid in this work. Then began the conjuration. I was not expecting the way it would affect me. Recalling it is even getting me a little emotional. It started like any other conjuration, just like all the other invocations of the day. Then about 1/3rd of the way through the sound sort of deafened in my ears and I started to feel very emotional. Tears slowly started to well up in the corners of my eyes and it was awe-inspiring. When I finally got to Michael's name, I choked, like one does when they're trying to talk while crying.

I was amazed and overcome. I gathered myself together and continued the conjuration still crying, but pulling myself together until I finished the conjuration. As soon as I was done, I started the conjuration again immediately. I was determined to recite it without being interrupted by tears. I had a better hold on myself, now, though still with watery eyes. It was incredibly powerful.

Half way through the conjuration I heard a loud pop and noticed that one of the candles situated on the railing for lighting and ambience had literally burst, shooting the lit candle from the bottle holding it. Hot wax exploded all over the floor. I had four other wine bottles with candles in them, and none of them shot their candle out.

I finished the second conjuration and did a third. Then I prayed whole heartedly to Michael from my heart. After the prayer, I put frankincense on the coals, and dangled the Ring of Solomon in the smoke as I petitioned Michael to bless and consecrate this ring. I petitioned him to give it power, allowing me to command spirits and perform miracles like John Dee and Solomon before me. It was a very long ongoing and unbroken petition that just flowed from the heart and probably lasted around five minutes.

I finished the consecration and rubbed the ring with Archangel Michael oil. Then I lifted up the scrying bowl and set the ring upon the seal of Michael and placed the bowl back on top of it. The bowl has a small bubble like the punt of a wine bottle in its foot so it fit the ring perfectly under it and still remained flat and stable. Then I asked Michael to appear before me in the bowl and speak to me if he had any message for me. Then I sat down and meditated, gazing at the bowl.

After about a minute I felt the mental suggestion to pour some of the red oil of Michael into the bowl, so I did. Then I sat, gazing, until I felt the suggestion to pick up the grape-wood and stir the water and oil solution together, so I did. The water in the bowl turned a deep red. In silent contemplation I saw unusual motion in the bowl. The motion also brought the image of a small red angel in a few different spots. There wasn't much after that.

I decided to thank Michael for his presence tonight and for consecrating the Ring of Solomon. I told him if he had any message to convey that he might do so in my dreams when I slept. I closed the ritual, then walked downstairs, leaving the ritual space entirely. On the landing I found that one of the candles had burned out leaving one of the strangest wax formations I have ever seen. I can't even begin to understand how the wax formed the way it did. It was in the shape of a crowned angel with spread wings hugging the top of the bottle. I don't do was interpretations but this image was unmistakable. It was truly baffling. This candle was the final candle between the ritual space and the ground floor. The placement gave particular pause. It was striking. An absolutely awesome way to close the ritual. The ritual ended a few hours ago and I am still buzzing. There is very much an electrifying sort of euphoric afterglow to such a powerful ritual. It's nice just to bask in and praise God."

    The first point of interest to note is the ancestor ceremony. His performance of the rite used different spiritual powers to access the dead. As long as it addresses the dead and those powers as needed it can work for the ritual. His completion of the ritual invited Michael to speak to him through dreams. For some spirits we would not want to invite them to access us in such a potentially intimate way. Dreams, are not however, the closest way into our minds. Spirits can meet us in dreams through a space in between theirs and ours. While our advice at the beginning of this was to develop a relaxed alertness, spirit magic can also be engaged through conjuring spirits to meet us in dreams, or meet us in a space between sleeping and waking. Finally, the wax figure. One of the fun elements of magic is the sort of spillover, the way in which things coalesce and spring up around the work we're doing. We find things that happen which assist us in strange situations and contexts. Items we need appear or pop up coincidentally or even in spaces where they simply shouldn't exist. Small acts and occurrences related to the goal we've sought, or related to the forces we've called upon work their way into our lives and show us the powers we've called percolating into our lives.

    Similar to this, small or bizarre physical occurrences which show spirit presences. Increases in wind, bursts of flame, crashing thunder at particular points in a conjuration might signal a spiritual presence. Spirits knocking out power to a building, breaking or dropping things, causing bizarre noises, or moving objects are all modes of physical manifestation by which a spirit may interact. I once had a scrying crystal shoot off an altar and roll over to my feet while I was using a talisman related to the angel I had last called into the crystal. In Alexander's account we have the angel leaving him a gift. A wax figure. Usually when people divine by means of wax forms the wax looks like a puddle. It rarely has any figurative shape. I saw a picture of his wax. It was crude but distinct and recognizable. It looked not unlike a child's clay sculpture of an angel.

    The day after the conjuration Alexander reported feeling "floaty, lofty, and peaceful." He was intending to use the house blessing spell using the Jupiter pentacle. He realized he should continue his focus on consecrating the ring and not on an additional spell. He set on a regimen of prayers to Michael and suffumigation until his St. Michael candle burned down.

    During the course of this time he had situations which inspired work with the dead. He had only begun exploring ancestor work in the preceding six months. Once he started working with the methods in *Luminarium* the effects of contact increased. He was visited by a particularly important ancestor in a dream and had several occurrences related to that ancestor. A child in his extended family made a reference to this ancestor, which brought Alexander concern. So, Alexander asked Hermes, his ancestors and his Guardian Angel to help this ancestor. He didn't have anything immediately happen. The next day he worked again at Sunrise using Greek Magical Papyri methods, work with his Guardian Angel, and the psalms to continue working towards the consecration of his ring. That night he had a dream in which the ancestor in question came and spoke with him, but he couldn't remember what he said. This led to greater concern.

    I recommended that he try a conjuration of Gabriel like Jonathan had done. He attempted the conjuration using the method from *Luminarium* combined with PGM IV. 2785-2890 (A spell from the fourth papyrus in the Greek Magical Papyri occupying lines 2785-2890). Instead of Gabriel he used *Luminarium* as a structure in which to call upon Selene and Hekate. This illustrates how the system can be modified to work as an over all structure for spirit magic.

    Like with many examples of people attempting magic with this structure he had a few things that occurred to him as he performed his ritual. First, he now owns the cat of the deceased relative in question, and lives in that relative's former home. The cat typically avoids his magical workings and heads to another room. This time the cat came into the room and went to the altar to sniff the candle representing its former owner. Then his phone, which was locked and set to silent over on his bed opened and spoke on its own. Its message, perhaps typical for a phone, clearly encapsulated the goal of his ritual: "I'm sorry I didn't hear that, could you repeat what you said." The final occurrence indicating a presence was a popping spark from the candle illuminating the ritual as he called upon Selene. Alexander felt that more weird things occurred than he typically experienced in impromptu on-the-fly magic; the weird things in this case helped clarify for him that his ancestor was ok, and therefore really provided the answer he wanted from the ritual.

 As for the requested dreams, Alexander said he typically has three to six dreams a night. Normally he wakes up for a minute or so after each one. He has a fair amount of awareness and lucidity regarding his dreams. After conjuring dreams from Selene, he woke several times through the night as normal. His awareness of his dreams was that they were empty. Less that he could not remember them so much as that they were simply blank. The space of the dream occurred but the dream was empty.

 I suggested to him that sometimes when a message is too much it will not immediately be visible and will begin to reveal over a few days. He noted that he specifically asked for a message in his dreams if the ancestor had an issue with which he needed help. A lack of issue could also explain the empty spaces. He decided he would pursue divination while working his normal Hermes devotions. The divination suggested all was well.

Angels and ministers of grace defend us!
Be thou a spirit of health, or goblin damn'd,
Bring with thee airs from heaven, or blasts from hell,
Be thy intents wicked, or charitable,
Thou com'st in such a questionable shape,
That I will speak to thee.

- Hamlet, by William Shakespeare

Printed in Great Britain
by Amazon